Knockers

Seekers

Askers

I ASKED

Turning Challenges into Triumphs

(It Is about Choices)

Carolyn McMillon

ISBN 978-1-64028-777-8 (Paperback)
ISBN 978-1-64028-779-2 (Hard Cover)
ISBN 978-1-64028-778-5 (Digital)

Christian Faith Publishing, Inc.
296 Chestnut Street
Meadville, PA 16335
www.christianfaithpublishing.com

Unless otherwise indicated, all Scripture quotations and Bible stories are taken from the New King James Version of the Bible.

Printed in the United States of America

ASKERS, SEEKERS, AND KNOCKERS

Matthew 7:7-8

****

**A.S.K. AND CHANGE YOUR LIFE
CREATE YOUR OWN PERSONAL JOURNEY TO SUCCESS
THROUGH DELIBERATE, INTENTIONAL ACTS**
Going from where you are today to where
you want to be tomorrow

Carolyn Jean McMillon

I dare you to come and take this journey with me.

This book is dedicated to the memory of my father and mother, Roy McMillon and Lillie Lee Fitzpatrick McMillon, for the strong work ethics they imparted to their children.

To my daughter Lillie Marque Stovall Walker, who thinks I am a rock star, for her unconditional love, support, and encouragement.

To my two grandsons Joshua Lee and Caleb Lee Walker for keeping me energized and grounded.

To the children of Roy and Lillie McMillon, my sisters and brothers:
Carrie Mae McMillon (in memory)
Tommy McMillon (in memory)
Minnie Lee McMillon Davis
Lula Mae McMillon Jackson
Mary Etta "Rosetta" McMillon Hampton
Roy "Royal" McMillon, Jr.
James McMillon
Bobby Lee McMillon
Bernice McMillon Warren (in memory)
Sylvester McMillon (in memory)
Me, no. 11 (Carolyn Jean McMillon)
Myles Lee McMillon
Magdlean McMillon Stayton
Geneva McMillon Pickens
Blanch Marie McMillon Gilbert
Baby Girl McMillon (in memory)
Dorothy Jean McMillon Shipp

And to everyone with dreams and visions and the courage to pursue them!

Carolyn McMillon is the daughter of poor share-croppers who overcame insurmountable challenges that led her from poverty living to break through the glass ceiling of the federal government's Senior Executive Service (SES).

SHE IS A FIRST-GENERA-TION SUCCESS STORY.

- The eleventh of seventeen children
- The first of her siblings to graduate high school
- The first and only one of her siblings to attend college
- The first and only one of her siblings to attend graduate school
- The first and only one of her siblings to have a professional career with the federal government
- The first of the entire McMillon linage to break through the glass ceiling to attain the rank of Senior Executive Service (SES) in the federal government

"Few times in a generation does someone come along with a way of looking at a question as old as, 'Why do so many people hold themselves back from the success they're capable of?' and come up with an answer that is at once so simple and yet so powerful."

—Jack Canfield
Originator of the 100 million-copies-sold
Chicken Soup for the Soul® series

Contents

Acknowledgments

Writing this book has been a humbling and transforming life experience. It has been my pleasure to share with you my path to success, both personally and professionally. It has not necessarily been a traditional path, but it is what has worked for me. I acknowledge that the most powerful influence in my life has been my relationship with my Creator who has led and directed me with great wisdom in all things.

To Brendan Westpal, thank you for taking the time to listen to my ideas of what I wanted in a logo and for taking those ideas and bringing them to life in the triangular design of Askers, Seekers, and Knockers.

To my dear friend Brenda Dokes, who gave of her precious time to read this work and offer recommendations and words of encouragement.

To Ying Chen, thank you for your courage and your willingness to live life by taking advantage of all that it has to offer. Thank you for being an encouragement to all people, those with disabilities and those without disabilities.

To Alphonso J. "Ajaye'" Carter, thank you for the courage to pursue your dreams, to make the difficult choice to correct your life vision, to exercise discipline in your life, and to find peace with your life choices.

To my treasured friend Patricia Stanfield Harris, who has always believed in me, from doing home improvement projects to writing this book. You have never failed to encourage me in all of my endeavors.

To my core members of Askers, Seekers, and Knockers (ASK), thank you for your friendship, your encouragement, and your exhortations. I am so proud of you and so thankful for your willingness to seek out your "true north" and take your own success journeys.

To my readers, it is my hope that through my journey and the vignettes of the lives of other individuals, you will find the inspiration and courage to change what should be changed in your life, to reach out, touch and make a difference in the lives of others so that you may impact the generation that is following after you. It is my hope that you will dance the dance of joy and, most important of all, to A.S.K. and keep Asking, to keep Seeking, and to keep Knocking until your goals are achieved and your journey is complete!

Part One: What Do You See?

- Introduction
  - Book Style & Presentation
  - Structured Learning
  - The Journey of Discovery is not an Overnight Process
- My Purpose for Writing This Book
- Define what Success Means to You
- Your Pre-Personal Self-Assessment— Where Are You?

Introduction

We were all born with a certain degree of power. The key to success is discovering this innate power and using it daily to deal with whatever challenges come our way.

—Les Brown

Do you have the courage to see your life differently? This book is for you, the strong, the survivors who are able to take valley experiences and turn them into life-altering changes that can yield successes beyond what you could have asked or imagined. This book is for those who will not give up because of the obstacles and challenges of life but will instead use those obstacles and challenges as stepping-stones to excel in spite of the obstacles and challenges. This has been my story and the story of most successful people, and it can be yours too. Most of us have already realized that many of the limitations we face are created by us; therefore, we are gifted with the power within us to fix what is broken, to restore what has been stolen away, and to remove every barrier that is holding us back from the life we were born to live. This book is composed of the principles and practices that I learned from studying the lives and strategies of numerous successful people, and through the wisdom bestowed upon me by the Great Creator of the universes. However, more important than that, this book is composed of the powerful principles, concepts, and practices of Askers, Seekers, and Knockers (ASK) that I have learned and applied to my life. Further, this book demonstrates how the reader can apply the same practical principles, concepts, and practices of A.S.K. to change their life, transforming them from the place where they are today in their life to where they want to be tomorrow.

Everybody can change anything about their life that they choose to. Take my life for example. I was not born a member of the privileged class; in fact, it was quite the contrary. If you knew the full story of my life, you would quickly realize that I would have been labeled as just another statistic and identified as not having a great chance at success. I was born a plain and simple country girl, child number 11 out of seventeen children. My parents were struggling sharecroppers. Neither of my parents graduated from school, but they were strong, hardworking, God-fearing people who taught their children strong work ethics. I learned at an early age that the life of a child of a sharecropper is not an easy life. My life was filled with early mornings, hard work, challenges, taking care of farm animals, tending household chores, and working in the fields in a household where there was little focus on education. Growing up on a farm teaches you many life lessons; among them, I would rate the top three for me are dedicated **persistence, perseverance,** and **prayer,** or more simply put, the ability to continually overcome obstacles until you achieve success, as you define what that success is for you. I like to call these my personal three *P*s of inspiration. Don't get me wrong, I am in no way complaining about the tough life I had growing up on a farm. You see, it was the toughness of that life that taught me how to dream and to dream big. To dream about wanting more, wanting to be more, and to strive and fight for greater than what I could even imagine. My problem was, at that time, I did not know how to go about achieving my dream of being better or how to even define in real terms what a better way was.

As I grew older, I became more and more disillusioned with where I was in terms of success, my education, my career, and my spirituality. I began looking internally at myself and assessing and re-assessing where I was in life. I spent a lot of time reading and studying about successful people, about their challenges and what they did to overcome those challenges. I began to ask the question, "Why not me?" And I kept asking and asking and asking. I remembered the biblical parable taught to me as a child by my mother: "Ask and you shall receive, seek and you shall find, knock and it will be opened to you." Even though I didn't quite get it or know what that really meant, it always stuck with me like a sliver in my mind. The principles outlined in this book have worked for me, and I believe they can work for you to if you will allow them to.

As I applied the biblical principle of *A.S.K.* in my life, and with dedicated, persistent effort, things gradually began to change and take on different meanings. It was from this point the principles of Askers, Seekers, and Knockers emerged. Through these principles, my life has taken on a gradual, but profound change. I realized with great certainty that I wanted the life of an Asker, a Seeker, and a Knocker.

Through persistence, perseverance, and much prayer, *A.S.K.* has influenced my philosophies, work ethics, education, habits, faith, my integrity, and most profoundly, my career. *A.S.K.* is a three-letter word, but it has profound impact. I believe the art of *A.S.K.* is the major universal law of attraction for SUCCESSFUL living.

Askers, Seekers, and Knockers is not a book about a theoretical approach to success; rather, this book is about actual practical and common-sense principles that I applied to my life to change the path and direction that I was on. These principles allowed me to create a successful road map for a new journey that changed my circumstances and delivered me from a life that was destined for poverty-level thinking and living. I have used these principles as a corrective action plan in my personal life, my education, my career, my spiritual life, and in organizations and programs that I have been employed to manage and lead. These principles are geared toward leading change and leading people; they are results driven, and they will get you the RESULTS you desire if you exercise a good amount of stick-to-it-ness!

The principles of Askers, Seekers, and Knockers are not unique. Under examination I found that most successful people employ these types of practices. I am convinced that had I not followed these principles, I would not have achieved the level of success I enjoy today. Far too frequently many people accept whatever circumstances life throws at them, and it shows in their actions and thoughts, and it manifests itself in an attitude of "I can't" for a myriad of reasons. But you can change this level of thinking and turn things around in your life and the lives of those you impact.

BOOK STYLE AND PRESENTATION

For ease of learning, I decided to structure this book into ten major parts with different chapters that progressively build upon one concept after another. This book is not simply a passive read; it is designed to get the reader actively engaged in the change process for their life. **Part 1, "What Do You See?"** consists of four chapters, including the pre-personal self-assessment. This section introduces the book, explains my purpose for writing this book, and helps the reader begin the process of assessing where they are in their life, where they want to be in their life, and what it will take to get them to the place they want to be in life. This section also requires the reader to define what success means to them personally at this point in their life.

Part 2, "Positioning Your Life for Success," consists of four chapters that help the reader begin the process of figuring out who they are and what their purpose is for being here. The reader will be introduced to the idea of developing their own life purpose statement. This section will provide a more definite answer to what success is. It will illustrate the parable of Lo Debar and the necessity of not accepting low standards of living no matter whether it is their choices or the choices of others that brought them to the place where they are in their life.

Part 3, "Aligning Your Life with the Universal Laws of Success," consists of four chapters that teach the reader about the concept of becoming an Asker, Seeker, and Knocker. This section covers the basic universal laws of success and teaches the reader how to apply these laws to their life, helping them to understand that these laws will work as effectively in their life as they have for other successful people. This section also focuses on the powerful impact of increase gained through giving and investing in the lives of others.

Part 4, "Askers, Seekers, and Knockers Are Committed," consists of five chapters that emphasize an attitude and spirit of never giving up no matter what. This section teaches the reader about how choices (good or bad) can leave an indelible imprint on their lives. It also demonstrates the impact of goal setting, goal accomplishment, and how habits all work harmoniously to help keep the reader on their journey to success.

Part 5, "Askers, Seekers, and Knockers Are Unstoppable," consists of five chapters that guide the reader through the process of recognizing their greatness and how to defeat self-defeating beliefs that may be holding them captive. This section also reinforces the principle that it is their responsibility to take charge of their own life and use their adversities as stepping-stones to greatness.

Part 6, "Askers, Seekers, and Knockers Accept No Excuses," consists of five chapters that teach the reader about breaking down artificial barriers, getting rid of excuses, and setting high-expectations that strengthen growth and development. This section reinforces the principle that there is no growth in the comfort zone and no comfort in the growth zone. This section encourages an attitude of high performance in the reader's personal and career life.

Part 7, "Askers, Seekers, and Knockers Care," consists of five chapters focusing on the valuable life principles of being a caring individual. It teaches the reader the importance of being a reliable, responsible, and trustworthy person of integrity that others can rely on.

Part 8, "Askers, Seekers, and Knockers Have Great Faith," consists of two chapters that teach the reader about drawing on their deep inner faith and becoming fearless in the face of difficulties. This section reinforces the realization that everyone should frequently tap into a greater source of power for strength and courage.

Part 9, "Askers, Seekers, and Knockers Are Dreamers," consists of a powerful chapter where the reader will be introduced to the power of dreaming. Through this process, the reader will learn the importance of harnessing the power of vision, discipline, and peace, which are necessary elements to accomplishing their dreams.

Part 10, "Awakening to Take Action," consists of five chapters and charts. This section teaches that a dream and a plan are nothing without execution. In this section the reader will learn how to pull together the results from the pre-personal self-assessment, the post-personal self-assessment, and the results from their personal individual actions to create goals and objectives which are critical for developing their overall personal plan of action. This is their road map of goals and objectives for their own personal journey to a life of success, as the reader has determined what that success is for them.

STRUCTURED LEARNING

Because we all learn and retain information differently, I have utilized several different methods to enhance the learning experience of the reader. First, there is solitary learning. Through this process the reader will learn on their own through self-study by simply studying the written word of this book. Second, there is reflective learning. Through this process the reader will utilize assessments, reflections, and meditations to discover more about themselves. This will allow the reader to take time for concentrated analysis in order to think more critically about past experiences and how they can use those experiences as building blocks for a more successful life.

Third, there is learning through storytelling. Through this process the reader will learn through others' personal journeys to success. They too faced the same or similar insurmountable obstacles, but they did not give up on their dreams. They kept striving until they overcame their challenges. These short vignettes of personal stories will serve as proof points to the reader that as surely as these individuals overcame their life challenges and used their experiences as stepping-stones to turn their lives around, so can the reader.

Fourth, there is retention through repetition. Through this process the various concepts about taking responsibility for one's own success is repeated for reinforcement. Retention through repetition is a concept we were all taught in early childhood education, and it is as relevant today as it once was. Repetition creates a rhythm of awareness in the reader that will help them retain the knowledge learned in this book.

Fifth, there is active learning. Through this process the reader will deepen their learning by creating personal individual actions aimed at eliminating negative behaviors and implementing new behaviors as the reader charts out a new journey for success. Finally, the reader will develop an overall personal plan of action designed to move them from where they are today to where they want to be tomorrow.

THE JOURNEY OF DISCOVERY IS NOT AN OVERNIGHT PROCESS

If you are not satisfied with the circumstances of your life, YOU are required to change them. Only you can change things! This book alone cannot change things for you, but through your persistent personal individual actions, you will come to realize that it can help you change your course. You can fix and restore that which is broken, that which is lost, and that which has been stolen away from you. This book alone cannot bring purpose to your life; however, it can help you establish the framework for you to discover your own purpose. You cannot wait for someone else to create or find your purpose; only you can do that. This book alone cannot bring you joy, happiness, or peace; however, it can help you become more productive so that you may be able to live a more fulfilled, satisfied, and joyous life.

This book can help inspire and motivate you to get involved in bringing about the change you seek. If you are willing to get involved in this process, you can find great satisfaction, which can bring a greater amount of overall enjoyment to your life. As you step out on this new journey to success, your motivation must be greater than a simple desire for more money and other material wealth. Although these are great considerations, your drive and motivation must come from a place deep within you to connect with the real you. This journey has to be about you becoming the person you were born to be.

As you assess yourself and look internally to begin the process of realizing who you are and who you are destined to become, you will realize that your greatest motivators/assets are the intangible qualities that make up the inner core of you. These are your dreams, visions, and desires. Those things that quicken your spirit and ignite your life. Those things that make you feel alive and valued, and those things that connect you to your passion and purpose.

As you read this book, one thing will be become apparently clear, and that is life is about choices. Will you choose today to change the circumstances of your life? This is the question I pose to you. Undoubtedly, you will not find any new information here that you have not heard before; the difference is, will you finally decide to choose differently? Will you start today to make the changes necessary that will guarantee you a life of abundance and extraordinarily successful living? That choice is yours to make. I hope you will choose to apply the lessons in this book to change your life. I challenge you to join me in becoming an Asker, a Seeker, and a Knocker.

My Purpose for Writing This Book

> Whatever we are now is the result of our acts and thoughts in the past; and whatever we shall be in the future will be the result of what we think and do now.
>
> —Author Unknown

I was motivated to write *Askers, Seekers, and Knockers* because I was driven with a deep inner desire to share with others what I have learned about the key to living an extraordinarily successful life and that it is possible for everyone. Your beginning does not necessarily dictate your end; it does not matter that you may have started out in life with a significant number of obstacles in your path. These obstacles can become your stepping-stones to a higher level of living. I am a first-generation success in my family.

In my studies of the lives of successful people, I find this to be the story of many successful people as they were the first in their families to break through the barriers of an underprivileged life to live a life that far exceeded the lifestyle of their parents and grandparents. Although I am the eleventh child out of seventeen children, I was the first child of my parents to graduate from high school, the only one of my sisters and brothers to attend college, the only one to attain a postgraduate degree, and the only one, so far, to have a professional career in the federal government.

This book provides a step-by-step guide for individuals who have a sincere desire to achieve greatness in their personal, academic, and professional lives. This book will help you realize that through the process of Asking, Seeking, and Knocking, you are capable of overcoming insurmountable obstacles that life presents. Success comes by positioning your life for success through recognizing the power of living in concert with the Great Creator's universal laws of success, by changing the way you think, by changing your behaviors, and by taking positive <u>personal</u> <u>individual</u> <u>actions</u> directed at achieving success.

Whether you have accomplished your educational goals, failed in that attempt, or are just now returning back to school, whether you are employed, underemployed, or unemployed, whether you are an office worker, a laborer, or an executive, whether you are married, divorced, or a single parent, whether you are in a difficult situation, coming out of a difficult situation, or heading into a difficult situation, this book is designed to help you position your life to overcome your challenges and achieve control and success over your undesired circumstances. Everyone has the ability to achieve and live a life of success where his or her personal and career goals are accomplished, and a life where they can live in a state of joy and satisfaction regardless of life circumstances.

I ASKed (Askers, Seekers, and Knockers) is designed to strengthen, encourage, and inspire you to take the necessary <u>personal</u> <u>individual</u> <u>actions</u> that will break down barriers, internal and external, and raise your level of expectations and beliefs so that you can have what life has to offer and to live the life you were born to live. The advice and information contained in this book are based on principles that I have applied to my own life and from information gleaned from professionals and experts who too turned their lives around to achieve greatness. It was the application of the principles found in this book that brought me from an underprivileged lifestyle to a life of extraordinary successes. I climbed from living in subsidized government-assisted housing to buying and selling several homes, each one successively better than the one before.

This book represents real accountings of my life and the lives of other individuals who have lived the life of an Askers, Seeker, and Knocker and how these individuals moved their life from a state of mediocrity to extraordinary success by taking the necessary steps to change. A life of success requires dedication, a commitment to excellence, and continuously making good choices for self-improvement.

What this book does not do is promise you that living a life of success is easily attained. Success takes hard work, consistent and persistent effort, goal setting, focus, a spirit of "stick-to-it-ness," and sacrifice. Yes, I said it, sacrifice! There is a price to be paid for a life of successful living, and you must be willing to make the necessary sacrifices and pay the price. You may find some of the advice in this book to be a bit unorthodox from other success books because it forces you to identify who you are, assess and take a personal accounting of yourself, analyze your own assessment, identify your own weaknesses, and establish your own <u>personal</u> <u>individual</u> <u>action</u> plan for achieving success based on the results taking from your assessments. What this book does offer you are real solutions if you are willing to pay the price. Yes, this is going to be a lot of work, but you will find in the end that it is well worth it.

Before We Get Started, Define What Success Means to You

Take this opportunity to describe what success means and looks like to you. In your response, explain how you will recognize success when you achieve it. Do not describe what other people say success is or what success looks like to them. This is about you and you only. We will explore this more as you prepare your overall personal plan of action.

Your Pre-Personal Self-Assessment: Where Are You?

Taking a True Private Assessment of your life

> This above all; to thine own self be true. And it must follow, as the night the day, thou canst not then be false to any man.
>
> —William Shakespeare's *Hamlet*

In taking responsibility for your life, it is important to take an in-depth internal look at who you are and where you are in life. Sounds easy? Not so fast. I do not mean do a superficial look. This type of internal assessment requires honest soul-searching. This is not about correct or incorrect answers; this is about you. It is okay if you do not have the answers to these questions in the beginning. This is about understanding who you are and where you are in life. It is about starting a path of self-development to help you attain what you believe you deserve out of life.

Conducting the Pre-Personal Self-Assessment

Following this section is the pre-personal self-assessment survey which you should complete. Answer the questions in the survey as best and honest as you can. This personal assessment is your self-audit. This is an important first step to holding yourself accountable for where you are in life. Your responses are for you and only you unless you decide to share them with others. The self-assessment is a process by which you learn more about yourself. Don't be discouraged if you are unable to truthfully answer some of these questions. At the conclusion of the book, you will be asked to use the results from the pre-personal self-assessment, the post-personal self-assessment, and the personal individual actions to develop an overall personal plan of action for getting you from where you are to where you want to be in the future.

The purpose of this personal assessment is to start you thinking about your purpose for such a time as this that you were born into the earth. All of us were born with a piece of the puzzle for life as it exists for time that we now live. The question is, are you walking in that purpose? If not, why not? Perhaps you were born to be a firefighter, a secretary, a doctor, a machinist, a professor, a teacher, a farmer, a stay-at-home parent, a military member, a medical provider, an architect, a business owner, a minister, a real-estate agent, a computer guru, a writer, a bank president, an entertainer, and so on and so on. No matter who you are, you were born with a purpose. The Great Creator has placed the gift of purpose in each of us. We all have a purpose to fulfill, and that purpose is needed for this period, for this place, for this time that you exist in the earth. My pastor teaches that we are born at the right time, in the right place, and in the right family, and I will add, with the right purpose for what the world needs right now.

Whether or not you are successful in life can only be defined by you. Your success should not necessarily be measured in material assets or career aspirations but, rather, by whether or not you are living in your purpose. There is great satisfaction and joy associated with living as who you were born to be. Identifying these things can help you determine what is missing in your life and what you should do to turn your circumstance around. This assessment cannot, nor can any other assessment tool, tell you exactly who you are; only you can do that. Hopefully, this assessment and your responses can provide you with the insight you need that will help you make informed decisions about where you go from here to turn your life around and put it on the path to your success.

You will be asked to take a post-personal self-assessment upon completing this book. You will compare the two self-assessments to determine where gaps may continue to exists. Let's get started.

Enter the date of your assessment when you begin this project. Take a true inner look at yourself. Remember, this audit is for your eyes only unless you decide to share it. The choice before you is to take an honest personal accounting of yourself and to be brutally honest with your answers.

Pre-Personal Self-Assessment
Where Are You?

What Is Your Spiritual Name? Who Are You?

This is a discovery question that cuts to the core of the inner you. Try to answer this question without stating your given name, race, ethnicity, national origin, gender, profession, heritage, occupation, or any other status in life. Your true spiritual name is tied to your purpose, the reason why you were born. When you were conceived in your mother's womb, your name was placed deep in your spirit to be searched out by you. The search for your true spiritual name will take you on your personal journey of discovery. You will be required to search your heart, your spirit, and your life for this answer. Quietly look for the common thread that has always been present within you. It is the thing which vibrates your inner spirit and quickens your life energy. Don't worry if you cannot answer this question at this time. More will be revealed as you read through the book that will better prepare you to respond to this question as you take this new journey.

If you were able to answer the above question, list your spiritual name below. How and when did you discover the real you or your spiritual name?

_____

_____

Personal Aspirations: Where Are You and Where Do You Want to Be?

1. Where are you physically—your location (state, city, neighborhood, etc.)?

   _____

         Is this where you want to be? _____ Yes _____ No
   If not, where do you want to be? _____

   _____

   What is holding you back from being where you want to be?

   _____

2. Where are you emotionally? _____
         Is this a good place for you? _____ Yes _____ No
   If not, where do you want to be emotionally? _____

   _____

   What is holding you back from being where you want to be?

   _____

3. Where are you spiritually?
         Is this where you want to be? _____ Yes _____ No
   If not, where do you want to be spiritually? _____

   _____

   What is holding you back from being where you want to be?

   _____

4. Where are you in your personal life (married, divorced, single, with children, etc.)?

   _____
   _____

   Is this where you want to be? _____ Yes _____ No
   If not, where do you want to be in your personal life? _____

   _____
   _____

   What is holding you back from being where you want to be? ___

   _____

5. Are there relationships in your life that you should change?
   _____ Yes _____ No

   If yes, why should they be changed? _____

   _____

   What is holding you back from making this change? _____

   _____

6. Are there relationships in your life that should be restored or established?
   _____ Yes _____ No

   If yes, why are these relationships important to you? _____

   _____

   What is holding you back from establishing or restoring these relationships? _____

   _____
   _____

Academic Aspirations: Where Are You and Where Do You Want to Be?

7.   Where are you in your academic life? _____
            Is this where you want to be? _____ Yes _____ No
     If not, where do you want to be? _____
     _____

     What is holding you back from being where you want to be?
     _____
     _____

Career Aspirations: Where Are You and Where Do You Want to Be?

8.   Where are you in your career/professional life? _____
            Is this where you want to be? _____ Yes _____ No
     If not, where do you want to be? _____
     _____

     What is holding you back from being where you want to be?
     _____
     _____

Financial Aspirations: Where Are You and Where Do You Want to Be?

9.   Where are you in your financial circumstances?
            Is this where you want to be? _____ Yes _____ No
     If not, where do you want to be? _____
     _____

     What is holding you back from being where you want to be?
     _____
     _____

Giving Aspirations: Investing in the Lives of Others—Where Are You and Where Do You Want to Be?

10. Are you predisposed to helping others such as participating in charitable giving, tithing, volunteering, etc.?

    Is this where you want to be? _____ Yes _____ No
    If no, do you feel it is not important to give your time, energy, or money to help others? Explain why or why not.

    _____
    _____

    What is preventing you from giving/investing in the lives of others?

    _____

If this assessment reveled that your life is not what or where you want it to be:

- Have you counted the cost (tangible and intangible) of getting your life on the track you want it to be on?
- Have you counted the cost (tangible and intangible) of not getting your life on track with what you want?
- Assess which cost is greater.
- Does the greater cost impact others besides you?

Keep your pre-personal self-assessment in a safe place and revisit it from time to time. Remember, this is for your eyes only. Share your audit only when you feel confident and safe enough to do so. We will revisit this pre-personal self-assessment after you finish reading the book.

At the end of each major segment of this book, you will be asked to complete a personal individual action related to that section. Don't ignore this project as it will become instrumental as you complete your overall personal plan of action.

Four things will be important as you set out to develop your overall personal plan of action for your personal journey of success:

- Pre-personal self-assessment
- Personal individual actions
- List of goals and objectives
- Post-personal self-assessment

Date Completed: _____

Part Two: Positioning Your Life for Success

- Figuring How Who You Are
- Discovering Your True Purpose
- Success Defined
- Success Does Not Live in Lo Debar

Figuring Out Who You Are

> If you do not know who you are, where you are, or where you are going, you may pass yourself on the pathway of life and never recognize yourself.
>
> —CJM

I once had a university professor who challenged me to identify who I am without giving my name, race, gender, status in life, or what I did to make a living for myself. I could not answer the statement. No one had ever asked me such a thing before. As I pondered this statement, I came face-to-face with the realization that I was only able to identify myself by using external identifiers, tangible things that could be seen in one form or another. What my professor was asking me to do was to take an in-depth internal look at the very core of myself. Needless to say, my professor did not answer the question for me. When I was unable to respond, she went on to say, "Carolyn, when you can answer that question, you will know who you are and who you were born to be."

At the time my professor posed this statement to me, I was a divorced single parent, living in government-subsidized housing, struggling to put myself through college, and barely living at poverty level. I hadn't a clue about how to identify myself without using external identifiers to describe or introduce myself. That question challenged me. It took me many, many years to come to terms with that statement and to understand the full impact of what it really meant. This statement is at the very core of what this book is about—knowing who you were born to be, what your purpose is for such a time as this, and setting your life on the pathway for you to get from life all that you desire and deserve.

Pondering this statement is what led me to the principles outlined in *Askers, Seekers, and Knockers*, in short, the law of ASK. Most of us were taught about the power of asking through studying the Holy Bible.

> Ask and it will be given to you; seek and you will find; knock and the door will be opened to you. For everyone who asks receives; the one who seeks finds; and to the one who knocks, the door will be opened. (Matthew 7:7-8, Ask, Seek, Knock)

ASK is a three-letter word with profound impact. Keep this universal law in mind; you will see it often throughout this book. This universal law has been in full operation in the earth since its inception, but not everyone is in tune with knowing how to apply it to his or her life. What I have come to learn is that for almost every challenge we face in life, there are three phases that we should go through—Asking, Seeking, and Knocking—in order to come out successfully on the other end.

Many people live in turmoil because they have never discovered who the real person is that they were born to be. Where people lack knowledge of themselves, lack a clear vision of who they are, lack self-identity and knowledge about the direction for their life, there is little to no growth and, often, much devastation. Your success and prosperity is tied to having a clear concept of knowing who you are and whether or not you are living the life you were born to live. As you go through this book, you will need to invest in a journal which you will use to record your journey. This can be a regular paper tablet, an electronic tablet, a notebook with loose-leaf paper, or a store-bought journal.

Personal Individual Action: We Become What We Think About

As human beings we have been given the power to control our thoughts and to fix what is broken in our own lives. For the next two weeks, take at least thirty minutes of quiet time each day (more if you can squeeze it in) for reflection and meditation.

For this first exercise, I want you to ponder on the critical questions, "Who am I, and who was I born to be?" Try to focus on an intangible, positive common thread that has always been present in your life. Listen to your inner spirit and what it may be saying to you. Use this time to encourage yourself and to meditate on that which gets you excited about life.

Answer these questions. Are you engaging in behaviors and habits that are moving you toward the person you were born to be, or are you engaging in behaviors and habits that are moving you farther away from the person you were born to be? Record your thoughts.

ACTION GOAL

Record at least one thing (more if you can) that you can start doing today that will help you to become the person you were born to be. Record at least one thing (more if you can) that you will stop doing today that will help you become the person you were born to be.

Where does this fit within your personal self-assessment (personal, academic, career, financial, and/or giving aspirations)?

Discovering Your Purpose

> My Life's purpose is to inspire and encourage others to reach their
> greatest potential by restoring that which was lost or stolen away so
> that they and the generations to follow may live a more joyful life.
>
> —CJM

Every life has purpose, and yours is no exception to this rule. Your purpose is the answer to the question, "Why?" "Why am I here? Why was I born for such a time as this?" Actually, the answer to the question of what is your purpose is a simple answer when you put careful thought to it, and it is the same for every single one of us. No matter what your calling is in life, your true purpose is tied to service. We are called to serve mankind through serving one another, to serve our families, our communities, our places of worship, and our nation. Through service, we connect to and accomplish our purpose for being.

Each person has the gift of service; we are all created with a servant spirit whether we realize it or not. Our service to one another is interconnected, interdependent, interrelated, and mutually dependent upon each other. We easily see the servant spirit prominently displayed in the call for military service, firefighters, medical providers, law enforcement, teachers, civil servants, parents, ministry workers, restaurant workers, inventors, carpenters, and other service providers. I challenge that you would be hard pressed to find anyone operating in a worthy goal who was not serving the needs of others. Remember the old saying, "No man is an island." Well, that is as true today as it was when this quotation was first uttered. The greater question to be answered is, "How is my service connected to my purpose?" And therein lies the rub. While we all have the common purpose to serve, we all will serve differently. And that is where our purpose in life comes alive and it becomes real to us.

As we struggle to understand our purpose, we come to the realization that it is impossible for any person to have a clear understanding of who they are and who they were born to be without comprehending their purpose. I believe everyone is born with a purpose. From the moment you were conceived in your mother's womb with the spark of life that was generated by the coming together of your mother's egg with your father's sperm, the Great Creator gave purpose to your life. Your purpose was hidden within you, and you alone must discover what that purpose is. It does not matter whether your existence was planned or unplanned—you have purpose. It does not matter if your mother or your father was not present in your life—you have purpose. It does not matter if you were born in or out of wedlock—you have purpose. It does not matter if you were born into a wealthy family, a middle-class family, or a poor family—you have purpose. It does not matter whether you were wanted by your parents or unwanted by your parents—you have purpose. Before proceeding any further in this book, you must be clear on this one single fact, and that is **YOUR LIFE IS NOT AN ACCIDENT AND YOUR LIFE HAS PURPOSE!**

Even if you were unplanned by your parents, you were not unplanned by the Great Creator of the universe, so accept this singular fact as the truth about your existence. The universal law of life requires two essential elements in human creatures, an egg and a sperm. It is no secret that when a female egg is introduced to a male sperm, life happens in living creatures, in most cases. The universal law of life has existed from the beginning of time. Thus, no matter what the circumstances were that brought your life into existence, it was no accident. When you come to terms and accept that your life has meaning regardless of your beginning, you will see that you serve a greater purpose than just simply being born; your life will take on a different meaning. You must realize that your purpose is bigger than your single life; it is more than your career, your hopes, and your dreams. You must understand that you were born to bring value to yourself, your family, your community, your profession, and every person's life that you encounter.

The most important journey you will ever embark upon is discovering, recognizing, and connecting with your purpose for being on earth, in this moment, in this time, in this space, and in this century. Until we connect with our purpose, it seems as though we are faltering and stumbling through life by happenstance. Searching for and connecting with our purpose is somewhat like using bumpers in bowling. Our purpose keeps us out of the gutters of life and keeps us in the game and on a somewhat straight path so that we have a fair chance to score in life. Without purpose, we seem to be pulled in different directions for different reasons. We are easily sidetracked and often make unwise choices that are life impacting. Connecting with our purpose brings joy, satisfaction, and fulfillment in both the major and minor things that we do in life. Connecting with your purpose brings clarity and understanding, and it helps to bring meaning to your life, and things begin to make more sense. When you connect with your purpose, the universe seems to cooperate with you. When you walk in your purpose, things and opportunities you have been chasing seem to start chasing after you, and that is a glorious feeling.

From the time you were formed in your mother's womb, you were set apart and appointed for a special need on earth. Each one of us carry within us a piece of the puzzle that the world needs. In order for you to successfully carry out your purpose for being here, you must position your life with that purpose, and when you position your life to line up with your purpose, you will live an extraordinarily successful life in all that you choose to pursue.

STORY TIME
My Story: Finding My Purpose, What Worked for Me

As I pondered the questions, "What is my purpose? What is my reason for being here? Who am I?" this truth came to life for me in the Book of Psalm 37:3-5: "Trust in the Lord, and do good …. Delight yourself also in the Lord, And He shall give you the desires of your heart … Trust also in Him and He shall bring it to pass." This passage hit me like a lightning bolt. My life took on a whole new meaning as I went on this journey of discovery. The most profound thing I learned was that these are instructions for my life and there are several fundamental principles wrapped up in that passage that I needed to come to a better understanding of before I would be able to grasp my life's purpose. I accepted that the Great Creator had already established purpose in my life and it was up to me to discover and connect to that purpose. I believed that my purpose was already hidden deep within my spirit, and I knew that in order for me to become my best self, I would need to walk out this journey of discovery.

As I spent time studying and learning about mankind's purpose, I came to realize that the desires of our hearts have less to do with material things, but are more focused on the intangible things of this life; so many people miss this point. They mistakenly think the above scripture refers to money, resources, homes, cars, and other tangible possessions. But, au contraire, through this process, I came to discover the great revelation that the desires of our hearts are our innermost yearnings, the core of our beliefs, intellect, awareness, innate abilities, and it is these intangible desires that drive our purpose and are intertwined with this miraculous thing called life. I recognized that these are the valuable characteristics that have been present in my life from the very beginning of my creation, and this is true for you as well. Through the quest of trying to understand my purpose, I came to value this concept as I realized that through my very own choices, I have the ability to change my circumstance. The more I lived by the principles of Psalm 37:3-5, the better I was able to uncover my true purpose.

WHERE TO START!

On purpose, you and I must strive to make good choices every day. Although, there will be some successes and some disappointments, don't give up. Fix what you can and do better with the next choice. Exercise your faith by believing that your plans will come to fruition. Going through this process taught me that timing is everything. "To everything there is a season, and a time to every purpose under the heaven" (Ecclesiastes 3:1). We all will go through different seasons in life, and it is easy to get discouraged and sidetracked as we are waiting for changes to occur in our lives. However, if we set a plan and stick with that plan, our goals will surely be accomplished. Getting your life on the success track will take time, so you should not get discouraged on this journey. Things may not happen the same way nor in the same time frame as with others that you may know. Nevertheless, stick to your plan and follow your own path. As you develop and apply these beliefs to your life, begin to examine your life through your own prism. Look inward and reflect on that inner yearning that creates the greatest passion in you. As you tap into this energy source, you will find your spirit may be quickened with subtle vibrations. You will come to realize that these intangible desires have been a common thread that has been present throughout your life, although you may not have previously recognized it to be so.

Discovering your true purpose will bring focus to your life. You will eventually be able to identify who you are without giving your name, race, ethnicity, gender, profession, or any other external factors. You will discover that your true name is present in your life purpose, and as you live through your purpose, you will also find your true name present in your personal and professional life. The most wonderful thing of all is that you will learn that as you connect with and begin to live in your purpose, you will come to realize that it will take care of you. Living in your purpose makes it possible for you to feed yourself, it will clothe you, it will sustain you, and it will make working at your profession no longer feel like work. Living in your purpose brings joy and passion and helps you fulfill your greatest desires.

As you proceed on this journey of discovering your purpose, you may find that your talent, skills, and abilities may not necessarily be your purpose. However, through your journey of discovery, you will find that your purpose is present in your talent, skills, and abilities. For example, you may find that you are quite gifted at singing, but singing may not necessarily be your purpose but your talent. You may find that it is through singing that your purpose lives. It may be that through singing you add value to your life and to the lives of others. You may find that your singing opens doors of significant opportunities and enables you to impact not only your life but the lives of many people.

YOUR PURPOSE IS NOT JUST FOR YOU

Take heed; your purpose should not be taken lightly as it should be used to bring about positive change. Ponder the following questions. Does your purpose positively impact others? Are the resources from your purpose used to invest positively in the lives of others, your community, and society as a whole? Are you using your purpose to positively influence the lives of others, or is it working to the opposite by bringing negative influence? These are the questions that must be addressed as you go on the quest of discovering your true purpose. The purpose for your life is not about material possessions and gains, albeit as you live in your purpose, you will enjoy an abundance of material possessions. Living in your purpose is about doing something that really matters; it does not matter how big or how small. Comprehending and living in your purpose brings value, meaning, vision, direction, motivation, hope, and focus to your life and the lives of others.

Although connecting with and learning to live out your life's purpose will help bring order and simplicity to your life, it is not a quick overnight process. This will take dedicated and deliberate study and effort. This is a lifelong process. You can expect challenges and some frustrations, and you may even face some criticism from those who know you are taking this journey; but don't you dare give up. Keep at it until you achieve results. Take time to journal your experiences and do not be afraid to talk with others whom you trust about your journey of discovering your purpose. As you acknowledge your purpose, don't be afraid to test your discovery with those whom you trust, and see if they will affirm your discovery. You were born with your purpose hidden within, and your journey is the discovery of that purpose.

Until you recognize and live in your purpose, you will never know how great you are. Unless you discover your true purpose for living, you will never know the real meaning of your life and discover all that you were meant to be. You will never take advantage of the opportunity to live the life you were actually born to live. You will never have the opportunity to touch the lives you were meant to touch with the impact it was designed for. The world will never truly receive the gift you brought to the earth. There are numerous books on the market that you may find helpful in the quest of discovering your purpose. However, I believe one of the most important books you should be sure to include in your library is the Holy Bible. Whether you agree or not, it does not make it less true that you were created by the Great Creator and he created you with purpose and for a purpose. In him we live and move and have our being (Acts 17:28)!

CREATING YOUR LIFE PURPOSE STATEMENT

Everyone should have a life purpose statement. This is the art of capturing in writing that which has always been present in your inner being. It is a single statement that puts into words the theme of your life—the reason why you exist. It captures the essence of why you feel so strongly about certain things. Developing your life purpose statement is equivalent to discovering a wonderful gift that you possess which should be shared with others. Don't rush the process. Be willing to invest as much time and energy as necessary for this process to evolve. The starting point of your greatest achievement is ignited at the point of your passion. Your passion is that which is created within you, and it is designed to connect with your purpose. Take an internal look inside of yourself, reflecting on your greatest achievements and the vibrations you experienced during those times.

Personal Individual Action: Start Where You Are

It is time to work on creating your life purpose statement. Set aside some time for reflection and meditation. Note that particular thing which gets you excited and quickens your spirit. It is as if your inner spirit vibrates when you connect with it. Close your eyes and concentrate on the real, internal, persistent desires of your heart. Ponder those thoughts, holding them in your mind and heart. Record those things you care deeply about; chronicle what is unique about you.

- Record your greatest desires.
- Record those things that you are most passionate about.
- Record your most unique qualities.

Connect with others. Seek out others whom you have confidence in, those who you believe will give you an honest and constructive view of what they see in you. Ask them what they see as the driving force in your life. Record what they say and how you feel about what they say. Examine whether this compares with what you see, feel, and believe about yourself. Don't be afraid to take advantage of the numerous resources available on the market to help you with creating your purpose statement if you need more help. Feel free to research these resources to help you practice writing your purpose statement.

ACTION GOAL

Use the above information to practice writing your life purpose statement. Try combining the information into a single statement about yourself. This is not a quick process. You will find yourself writing and rewriting this statement. Don't get discouraged. I am still tweaking mine.

Examples of Life Purpose Statements

"To inspire and encourage others to reach their greatest potential by restoring that which was lost or stolen away so that they and the generations to follow may live a more joyful life."

"To use my gifts and talents to encourage, educate, and provide opportunities to people with disabilities."

"To use my voice and my words to uplift and exalt."

"To use my talents, skills, abilities, and resources to educate, to train, and to encourage communities to continuously grow through restoration and volunteerism."

Record Your Statement

Where does your life purpose statement fit within your personal self-assessment (personal, academic, career, financial, and/or giving aspirations)?

Success Defined

> Achieving success is about acquiring wisdom, the application of understanding, and consistently making appropriate choices using that wisdom and understanding.
>
> —CJM

Defining What Success Means to You

As we get started on this adventure, it is absolutely important and necessary for you to define what success means to you. This is why you were asked to address this issue in the beginning of this book. Upfront let us settle one issue; this book is not about teaching you how to become a member of the "superrich club." Accept it, not everyone in this world will be rich and famous. Do not confuse success with wealth. Not everyone will be Bill Gates, Warren Buffett, the Koch Brothers, Christy Walton, or Oprah Winfrey. In fact, billionaires represent a very small percentage of the world's population. According to Forbes list of billionaires, the total number of billionaires represent about 1,800 individuals out of the total world population of over 323 million people. However, if you are ready to take a realistic look at your life and determine that you are ready to work at achieving the level of success that you desire, you are ready for this journey. If you are ready to move from where you are to where you want to be in life and if you have not achieved your highest potential, this journey is for you. If you are interested in turning your life around and putting it on track to achieving your highest level of success as defined by **YOU**, this journey is definitely for you.

SUCCESS DEFINED

What is success? *Merriam-Webster* defines success as a "favorable or desired outcome," "the accomplishment of an aim or purpose." However, I think it is interesting how Deepak Chopra defines success. He states, "Success in life could be defined as the continued expansion of happiness and the progressive realization of worthy goals." But, better still, the more relevant question is, What is success as defined by you? What does success look like to you? This is a question that must be answered by you. Success is a subjective term based on your own personal opinion, your personal views, your personal observations, and your starting point. You were intrigued to pick up this book because no matter what your current status is in your life, you desire more, or you would not have been attracted to this book. No one else should, nor will this book, define what success should be for you. All people, and you are no exception, must define their own level of success. Your success is personal to you, and you should not compare yourself to anyone else because your starting point for success is not the same as any other person. For example, success for me is not the same as the level of success for retired Army General Clara Adams-Ender, a sharecropper's daughter who rose up to become an army general. As I studied the life of Ret. General Adams-Ender, I found that we share some similarities in how we grew up, but success for us took two totally different paths. I encourage you to read her story in her book titled "My Rise to the Stars". I have chosen to measure my level of success beginning from the point of where I started out in life in comparison to where I have come thus far.

How I define success changes from time to time as I accomplish and establish new goals. When I achieve a desired worthy goal or level of success, I create a new goal, thereby continuously propelling my personal, spiritual, and professional life forward. My measuring stick is laid against my own personal definition of success and achievements. My point of origin is from that of a poor farm girl, the daughter of poor sharecroppers, living in a house on land that we could never hope to own, and in a family where education was not a top priority. I realize that what I measure as great achievements may seem commonplace to some individuals who do not bear my scars, did not face my challenges, and did not have to break down my barriers in their life. In like manner, you will have to do the same. Start from where you are. Start by visualizing what life will be like when you have your heart's desires. Any movement from where you are toward your desired outcome is a successful accomplishment. Simply set your mind to what you want to accomplish in every area of your life.

According to Stephen Covey, author of *The Seven Habits of Highly Successful People*, whatever your desires are for success, they are created twice. Your definition of success is first created in your mind's eye through the power of visualization long before you enter into the second phase of creation, which is the physical manifestation of your success. What Covey is explaining is that before you can experience outward success, you have to first experience inward success. You must first be successful in your own mind before success can manifest itself in your reality. Use your wonderful, marvelous, and powerful creative brain to visualize what you define as success for your life. Your mind will believe what you program it to believe, and your mind will accept as truth what you tell it is true, coupled with visualizations and mental images of that truth. Your body will follow where your mind leads you, good or bad. Through the power of visualization, we call those things that do not yet exist into existence. Through the power of visualization, we begin with the end in mind by mentally creating that which we desire. For example, if one of your goals for success is obtaining a graduate degree, you visualize yourself on graduation day, in your cap and gown, marching up on that platform and receiving that hard-earned degree in your hands. This visualization takes place long before you even start the application process. You clarify this goal in your mind's eye even more by determining what field of study you will enter, what school you will attend, and what financial resources you will procure to make this possible. You see what doors of opportunity will be opened to you with this degree, such as career advancement, more financial independence, a better and more upscale lifestyle. You continue to explore idea after idea, until you narrow your choices down to a plan of action to fill out and submit your application to the university of your choice. And suddenly, one day you step into the classroom and into the first day of achieving your graduate degree. You keep stepping into that classroom, you keep studying, you keep visualizing success until finally, one day you will step across the platform to receive your graduate degree. You started this process with the end in mind. You created and held the vision mentally, until the manifestation was physically achieved. Most successful people are visualizers—they see success, they feel successful, and they experience success long before they actually achieve success.

Your consideration of what success is for you will often be defined by looking from where you started out in life to where you currently are in your life and to where you desire to be. Your vision of success should consider the deficits that exist in your life and the barriers that are holding you back. Keep in mind that often the barriers that are holding you back are of your own creation—many are attitudinal and superficial. You must see yourself breaking through and breaking down those barriers. While no one can tell you what success should look like for you, I would only offer this word of advice: if you are healthy and capable, your ultimate level of success should be independent of reliance on or assistance or subsistence from a source absent your own abilities, contributions, or creations.

As you consider your ultimate level of success, don't be afraid to dream and dream big. We will talk more about dreaming later in the book. Do not let anyone or anything get in your way, and do not let anyone cause you to feel that you do not deserve what you want or that your ultimate level of success is too lofty. For example, if you define success as being a dedicated stay-at-home mother who will contribute to society by raising the next generation of healthy productive leaders, you should set your life goals toward that direction. If you aspire to become the next president of the United States, a congressman, a doctor, a member of the military, a writer, an educator, or a civil servant, visualize it and set out to accomplish it. Your definition of success will be used to guide you in developing your goals and objectives in your personal plan of action.

Success Does Not Live in Lo Debar

As you have read, this book is about taking responsibility for your own destiny. That being said, let me be the first to inform you that successful people do not live in Lo Debar because they cannot prosper there. No more playing the blame game and making it the fault of society, family, parents, or holding anyone else accountable for your circumstances in life. Successful people are successful because they do successful things every day one after another. They transform their thinking, they set goals, they graduate from high school, they go to university, they attain graduate and post-graduate degrees, they learn new skills and sharpen old ones, they hold themselves accountable, they hone their crafts, they pursue their desires and dreams, and they work hard at bringing those desires and dreams to a state of reality, and they do not live and remain in Lo Debar! I want you to understand the concept behind the term Lo Debar. Far too frequently people get trapped in an allegorical Lo Debar mentality and don't even realize it. In this book the term Lo Debar is used as a state of being that can be either a mental or physical state of being or both.

A Place Called Lo Debar

This story is found in the Bible, the Book of 2 Samuel 4 and 9. The story is about Mephibosheth, the son of Jonathan and grandson of King Saul. As the story goes, when Mephibosheth was about five years old, his father and grandfather were engaged in the Battle of Mount Gilboa, where they were overthrown and killed. Of course, the victors came looking for Jonathan's descendants, in this case Mephibosheth. In order to save Mephibosheth's life, his caregiver decided to run away with him. In her zeal to save his life, she ran so fast that she tripped and fell with him. When she fell, she dropped Mephibosheth, causing him to sustain two broken legs, which left him paralyzed from his waist down. Mephibosheth, being an invalid, was carried off, through no fault of his own, to a place called Lo Debar. This was a place of desolation, loneliness, poverty, and a place of hopelessness and despair. What was meant as a great gesture in trying to help him ended up dooming him to a life of poverty. Mephibosheth lived a major part of his life in a state of poverty in the house of Machir at Lo Debar, where he remained until King David rescued him.

The message of this story is that it was not Mephibosheth's fault that he ended up in a place of desolation and poverty; nevertheless, he was there. It also may not be your fault that you may have ended up in your allegorical Lo Debar. Perhaps you had an underprivileged childhood, you grew up without parents, you were deprived of a good education, you suffered abuse, you are divorced or widowed, you lost your job, you are underemployed, you were born with certain disabilities, you are currently homeless or in jail or prison, or that you are living in a state of abject poverty. Nevertheless, it is your fault if you remain in your Lo Debar. Too frequently, unsuccessful people accept their plight in life and use it as an excuse to remain where they are. They say things like, "I work very hard but just can't get ahead. You have to be in the right place at the right time. I am just not lucky. Doors were closed to me because of my race, gender, or disability, etc." This type of speech and limited beliefs are entrapments and serve only to keep you stuck in Lo Debar. Where you are today may be the result of your bad choices or wrong decision, or it could be the result of someone else's actions that brought you to Lo Debar. The good news is you do not have to remain under the curse of your own actions or the adverse actions of someone else's bad decisions. You have the power to identify what needs fixing and fix it.

When I reflect on the story of Lo Debar, I am reminded of the life story of Iyanla Vanzant. Today, she is a well-known and famous spiritual adviser, life coach, and bestselling author who has appeared on the Oprah Winfrey television show numerous times. However, this was not always Iyanla's story. This is a courageous woman with an astounding life history. When you study her story, you can certainly surmise that this woman found herself many times living in an allegorical Lo Debar. Some of these unfortunate choices were thrust upon her by others and some choices she made herself. She suffered a life of numerous challenges to include sexual abuse, obesity, single motherhood, living in poverty, and neglect. This is a miraculously strong and brave woman who turned her life struggles into numerous successes only to suffer the traumatic loss of a beautiful daughter, a divorce, the loss of a home, and other financial challenges. These life-altering events sent her life spiraling out of control and once again where she suffered tremendous losses and setbacks. One could say she found herself right back in Lo Debar.

Nevertheless, no matter what the circumstances were that brought Iyanla back to the place of an allegorical Lo Debar, she did not remain there. She did not waddle in her circumstance and strap on a permanent "woe is me" attitude and blame others for her troubles and misfortunes. With the help of friends, professionals, and many others, she fought her way back to success. If you have not had an opportunity to do so, I highly recommend that you study the inspirational life of Iyanla Vanzant, her struggles and her accomplishments. If you have found yourself living in an allegorical place called Lo Debar, you will find inspiration and encouragement by reviewing some of the numerous publications by this empowering author. I especially recommend her book *Peace from Broken Pieces: How to Get Through What You're Going Through.* You will also find strength in studying the personal individual actions Iyanla Vanzant took to put her life back on track.

Personal Individual Action: Get Out of Lo Debar

Set aside some time for reflection and mediation about your current circumstances. Starting today make a personal commitment to stop blaming anything or anyone for your current position in life.

Today you are no longer a victim of your circumstances! Go back and review your definition of what success looks like to you. Update your statement where appropriate and annotate the date you updated your statement.

ACTION GOAL

Create in your journal a personal victory statement focusing on your ability and the power you possess that will help you change your circumstances in life. Example, "Starting today, I will no longer accept that where I am is where I will remain. Today, I am changing my life for the better. I am making new plans!" Record your victory statement and list at least two things (more if you can) that you will start doing today that will set you on your journey to a successful life.

How does your new victory statement fit within your personal self-assessment (personal, academic, career, financial, and/or giving aspirations)?

Part Three: Aligning Your Life with the Universal Laws of Success

- Becoming an Asker, Seeker, and Knocker—ASK
- Askers, Seekers, and Knockers Are Accountable for Their Own Circumstances
- Finding Your True North Through Asking, Seeking, and Knocking
- Askers, Seekers, and Knockers Live, Work, and Prosper In Concert with the Universal Laws of Success

Becoming an Asker, Seeker, and Knocker: ASK

> Ask, and it shall be given you; seek, and ye shall find; knock, and it shall be opened unto you.
>
> —Matthew 7:7

Let us look at the principles behind Asking, Seeking, and Knocking, beginning with the basic definition for the words *ask*, *seek*, and *knock*.

THE ASKING PERIOD

Webster's Dictionary defines the word *ask* as "to request, to petition, to solicit, to require, to demand, to expect." Thus, I believe the Asking period is your personal assessment period. This is where you take personal responsibility for where you are in your life. You will accomplish this by asking yourself a series of questions. You will assess who you are and where you are in your life on many different levels. This is the period where you must come face-to-face with your challenges and the circumstances that you need to confront so that you may do something about where you are. The Asking period is about the choices you make, and it is a continuous process. This is the period of your life where you ask yourself what it is that you want, where you make demands on yourself, where you require yourself to become accountable for your actions, and where you raise your level of expectations for yourself. It is important to always assess and reassess where you are in life.

If you are serious about changing your circumstance, you must change your expectations and you can change your expectation by implementing Asking in your life. As you proceed through the Asking period, do not be afraid to demand an answer from yourself regarding your expectations. Remember, this is your private assessment of yourself and you do not have to share this information with anyone until you are ready. Therefore, you can be brutally honest with yourself. As you take a self-inventory of where you are, force yourself to face the challenges or the circumstances that you need to confront. Dare to believe and expect that you can expect the best for your life and for those whose life you touch. At this juncture of your life, you may be faced with numerous challenges such as single parenthood, a lack of an education, divorce, the loss of a loved one, the loss of a job, battling health issues, living in a shelter, and the list could go on and on. Nevertheless, you have the power to change where you are.

THE SEEKING PERIOD

Webster's Dictionary defines the word *seek* as "to go in search of, to try to acquire, to strive for, to try to reach, to discover, to locate." I believe the Seeking period is your period of preparation. This is where you identify what you need to do to bring success into your life. It is where you count the cost and make the necessary sacrifices. This is where you take control over your own circumstances. In the Asking period you identified things you needed to do to get your life on track. Seeking is when you set out on that adventure to exert the effort to acquire the goals you are striving to achieve. This period can be classified as your training and preparation period. This is where you discover the cost and the sacrifice that is required and what it will take to accomplish your goals. Not only do you count the cost of doing what is necessary to put your life on track. This is where you should take responsibility for exerting the cost of doing what is necessary, and this is where you count the cost of NOT doing the hard things to get your life on track. For example, there is a cost to be paid and sacrifices to be made when you decide to get an education, and there is a cost to be paid and sacrifices to follow if you choose not to get an education. The universe requires everybody to pay a price for doing and not doing. The universe does not allow anyone to slip by; therefore, you too must pay your debts to the universe.

THE KNOCKING PERIOD

Webster's Dictionary defines the word *knock* as "to strike with a hard blow, to collide with something, repeated taps; to make a great effort (exhaust oneself)." I believe the Knocking phase is your period of stepping out into the pathway of opportunity. You are now ready to knock on the doors of opportunity that awaits you. You identified what was necessary; you took on the challenges, made the sacrifices and payments of preparation, and now you are ready to move forward.

It's now time to apply for your dream job, ask for that raise and promotion that you have been working so hard for. Take that trip that you have been saving for. Accept the speaking engagement you have been waiting for. Submit your manuscript of the book to a publishing company. Set out on the path to receive the fruits of your labor. This is also a period when you could become discouraged. Knocking sometimes will require repeated tapping. It may mean going to multiple interviews, applying for multiple jobs, making numerous requests—but don't give up. Sometimes success is just around the next bend. Jack Canfield, the author of *Chicken Soup for the Soul* and numerous other publications, tells the story of his struggles when trying to find a publishing company to publish his first book. He stated that he and his coauthor, Mark V. Hansen, tried 144 times before they found a publishing company to take them on. Fight hard for your success and don't give up until you get what you want. When success comes, and it will come, take time to enjoy it. But don't get too comfortable because Asking, Seeking, and Knocking is a continuous process for achievement and improvement. When you accomplish one goal, it is time to prepare to start on a new one.

Askers, Seekers, and Knockers Are Accountable for Their Own Circumstances

> Man is asked to make of himself what he is supposed to become to fulfill his destiny.
>
> —Joshua Tillich

We are taught all of our lives that the most effective way to receive anything is to simply ASK. This is what the Asking, Seeking, and Knocking period is all about in our lives. We began by assessing who we are and who we were born to be. A true Asker's first step begins with the process of ASKing. As we discussed earlier, some of the most common questions that will probably surface first are centered around the "Why am I here? What was I born to do? What is my purpose in life?" questions. Surely, as you continue to ask yourself these series of questions, more and more answers will become apparently clear to you. Going through this process can be an exciting adventure that creates internal vibrations signaling your internal compass that you are on the right track. However, this can be a long and tedious process that requires profound, thought-provoking questions and pondering on information that can take you back as far as your childhood.

The Art of A.S.K. Is Present in Our Early Lives

Our Asking, Seeking, and Knocking really starts at a very early age. You see it in its most immature stages when children talk about what they want to be when they grow up. Parents should begin at this starting point to nurture and develop this enlightening spirit of Asking, Seeking, and Knocking in their children as they progress through life. When a child or adult makes the assertion that they want to accomplish a certain aspect of life, parents should explore those possibilities through a series of discussions. If the child says they want to be a teacher, a lawyer, a fireman, a soldier, and so on, their dreams should never be stifled. Not only should they dream, but they should dream BIG. Parents and mentors should encourage that aspiration with open-ended questions to get them talking even more about the possibilities. Ask questions and engage in conversations that excite the inner vibrations of excitement.

Through your mind's eyes, you can explore countless impossibilities and seek options for turning them into possibilities. Nurture the spiritual being by exploring inner thoughts and motivations. Do not be afraid to explore questions that deal with feelings about choices. Allow the spiritual part of you to act as your conscious guide; the more questions you raise about why you feel a certain way about a matter, the more possibilities will emerge. Raising your spiritual awareness is like a drop of water hitting a full body of water and creating a ripple effect. The more you ask and look inward, the more ripples are formed as possibilities; this can be a good thing.

All Askers, Seekers, and Knockers Go Through a Period of Personal Reflection

Examine where you are in life and where you want to be; if you do not like what you see, agree to change it. Ask yourself, "Am I who I want to be? Am I happy and satisfied with where I am at this stage of my life? Is my life on the right track, and do I know where I am headed?" An even greater question to explore is whether your family is on the right path, but that's a story for another book. If your life is unfulfilled, do not be afraid to apply the principles found in *Askers, Seekers, and Knockers*. As you walk through this accounting of your life, a word of caution: do not confuse the challenges you face in life as being on the wrong pathway. Even with the best choices and the best-laid plans, you will face challenges, uncertainties, and setbacks.

The purpose of this book is not to promise you a life of ease and trouble-free living. The purpose of this book is about *carpe diem*, seizing the day and capturing the opportunities of what life has to offer. It is about not letting life slip past you because of its challenges. It is about knowing how to pick yourself up and get back in the game of life when circumstances cause you to sometimes stumble and fall. It is about knowing that you know that you know your life is following the path that you were intended to follow in spite of all else. It is about not letting the storms and the winds of life blow you away. This book is about <u>Changing</u> <u>Your</u> <u>Circumstances</u> by becoming an Asker, a Seeker, and a Knocker! If you determine that you want to get from where you are to where you want to be, get the Nike spirit and just do it!

This book examines what happens as we go through the developmental phases of Asking, Seeking, and Knocking. The exercises in this book will hold you accountable for your own success or failures. As I stated earlier, no more finding fault by blaming your family, society, your boss, or the government for your general overall plight in life. This book will not allow you to blame others or make excuses for your failures. Although there may be reasons for your failures or setbacks, those reasons can no longer be your excuses for staying where you are.

My wish for you is that after reading this book, you will be moved to action. My hope is that you will initiate the action to assess yourself, to identify what should be changed in your life, and to develop a plan to put you on the road to great success so that you may achieve out of life what you believe you absolutely deserve. The good news is, anybody can apply the principles of Askers, Seekers, Knockers and get results, and that is true for you too. The more skilled you become in applying these principles, the greater the results in your life. I continually utilize these principles in my life even today. Asking, Seeking, and Knocking is a continuous self-evaluation process and should be applied to every major goal you set for your life.

Personal Individual Action: ASK

Set aside some private time to reflect and mediate on becoming an Askers, Seeker, and Knocker. Developing this skill will prove to be one of your more valuable assets. This process will help you live a life of continuous self-improvement.

ACTION GOAL

Did you discover any insights that you will apply to your life? Record your responses in your journal.

How does establishing the art of A.S.K. fit within your personal self-assessment (personal, academic, career, financial, and/or giving aspirations)?

Finding Your True North through Asking, Seeking, and Knocking

Asking, Seeking, and Knocking is a type of personal navigation process that will help you identify and find your authentic self. You are reading this book because somewhere and at some point in time you got off the correct path for your life that was driving you toward your "true north." Taking this journey will allow you to search for your *true north*—the real focal point of your life. As you assess your life, your value system, your relationships, and those things that hold real meaning for you, you should reflect on those ideals and values which ground you, root you, and give you a sense of a real foundation. Asking, Seeking, and Knocking is a continuous journey, not a destination, that keeps you on your life's track by pulling you toward your purpose. It keeps you looking and heading north. When you know who you are, what you value, and your purpose, you will be able to better set your life on the path to true success.

When I first set out on my quest of Asking, Seeking, and Knocking, Psalm 37:4, "*Delight thyself also in the LORD: AND HE SHALL GIVE THEE THE DESIRES OF THINE HEART,*" BECAME MY TYPE OF TRUE NORTH (italics added), my focal point. This is where my personal journey of Asking began. The more I studied this passage, the greater the vibrations in my inner spirit. Unfortunately, too many people confuse this passage with the tangible things of life. They think it refers to things, resources, or even people. However, I personally found that this passage is about so much more than physical possessions and material things. As mentioned earlier, I find that this passage is about our inner yearnings—the intangible things of life. It is about the deepest part of what we are most passionate about. The desire of our heart is a positive and focused energy that is deeply rooted in the very core of our existence. You will know it when you tap into that energy source of your true north, because it makes you come alive; it quickens your spirit. This is what you are most passionate about; it brings you joy, excitement, satisfaction, and productivity. It adds value to your life and to others whom you come in contact with, and ultimately, it can bring you prosperity.

When you learn to really connect with this energy, it will change your thinking and ultimately transform your life. When you identify this energy, you will recognize it as the common theme or common thread that has always been present in your life, hidden in your inner core. It is the path that has been with you all along just waiting for you to discover it, recognize it, tap into it, and use it. This is something so interconnected to you that it will actually make a living for you. It shows in your chosen career professions; it shows in your talent and your skills. However, it may need developing. It is your PURPOSE. Go ahead, ask yourself what it is that gets your inner spirit vibrating. Close your eyes, meditate, and think about your life.

STORY TIME
My Story: Finding My True North through
Asking, Seeking, and Knocking

This process of Asking, Seeking, and Knocking took years before I learned how to tap into my energy source. As I took an accounting of my life, I evaluated the types of jobs I was naturally drawn to, the types of commitments I volunteered for, the academic profession I chose, and the roles I naturally assumed in my family life. In the diversity of these roles, I discovered that without fail, I always chose jobs, volunteer opportunities, assignments, and roles where I was helping, restoring, creating, repairing, or bringing something into compliance with a standard. I realized that my passion and energy levels were off the charts when I was busy working, identifying, and assessing issues in problematic circumstances and finding solutions. I found excitement in assessing situations and programs, analyzing and identifying brokenness or identifying things that were out of compliance, and creating plans and solutions to correct brokenness in areas of noncompliance. I found my heart racing, my brain firing, and my spirit energized when I was working to bring some program, office, or system into compliance with established rules and regulations or planning family reunions. My energy levels were most high when I was working to find solutions, repairing, and restoring. This energy level was most pronounced when I worked with people issues and problems, providing guidance, mentoring, making recommendations, and recommending solutions to challenges.

I found this fact to be true from the time I was hired in my first job outside of the farm as a trimmer with the Van Heusen Shirt Company, to my first part-time job as a secretary with the Masonic Relief Association, to my first full-time secretarial job with the University of Arkansas at Pine Bluff, and throughout my career as a civil servant with the federal government. I find that guiding, leading, restoring, finding solutions, creating, mentoring, coaching, teaching, and bringing value to others is my *true north.*

When you actually connect to the *desires of your heart*, you will be following the path of your *true north.* Your *true north* will guide you toward what you were born to do, and if you allow it, it will fulfill you in the areas of your dreams—personal and professional. Helping others has always been present with me throughout my life. When I look back on the path of my journey even as a child, it was even present during playtime. When I am operating in my purpose, I find that the elements of guiding, leading, restoring, finding solutions, creating, mentoring, coaching, and teaching are always present in one form or another. I find joy, satisfaction, peace, and completeness, and I wish the same for you as you discover your true authentic self on this journey of discovery.

Personal Individual Action: Tapping into Your Personal Desires

Set aside some private time for reflection and meditation. Ask yourself a series of personal strategic questions that drive your spirit. Think about what you value and why.

ACTION GOAL

Record your response to the below questions in your journal.

- If you were free to do anything in life you wanted to do, what would it be?
- What would you be willing to sacrifice everything for?
- If you were forced to pick only one value to live by for the rest of your life, what would it be?
- If you did not have to work for a living, what would you choose to do five days a week for free simply because it brought joy, satisfaction, and value to others?
- What are the four most important things you will tell your family about that will help them live a joyful, peaceful, and fulfilled life?

Where does finding your *true north* fit within your personal self-assessment (personal, academic, career, financial, and/or giving aspirations)?

Askers, Seekers, and Knockers Live, Work, and Prosper in Concert with the Universal Laws of Success

> Most people search high and low for the key to success. If they only knew, the key to their dreams lies within.
>
> —George Washington Carver

Align Your Life with the Universal Laws of Success

The universal laws of success were created at the beginning of time by the Great Creator Himself. The laws already exist—right here, right now. They were put in the realm of the earth from the very beginning of life. You don't have to invent anything; you just have to live in accordance with them. All successful people do. The level of success we enjoy in life lies within the degree to which we align ourselves with and how we operate in accordance with these laws.

Everything that happens in our lives results from the consequence of either applying or ignoring these universal laws. Allow me to illustrate; let's examine the law of gravity. The law of gravity operates in the realm of the earth, and we must respect that law or we cannot successfully exist in the natural realm of the earth. Gravity is the force that holds the waters in the oceans, and it is the force that holds the moon in its orbit as it impacts the rise and fall of the tides. It is this invisible force that attracts all objects to all other objects. Everything you do is regulated and shaped by gravity. It prevents you from floating while you go about your daily routine, such as walking, sleeping, eating, or sitting. Gravity is so natural to us that we rarely give it a second thought, but it governs everything about us. It is important that we understand the principles of gravity, or it could cost us our very existence. Jumping out of an airplane without a parachute certainly would send you spiraling down to the earth with the realization that gravity is important to our survival. Because you understand that gravity is a force that attracts all objects to all other objects, you know that as soon as you step out of the airplane, gravity goes to work to attract your body downward toward the earth; thus, you would equip yourself with a parachute in order to guide your descent with a steady, controlled, safe speed until you are safely on the ground.

As with the rest of the universal laws, we live, work, play, survive, achieve success, or even fail depending on how we interact with the rules that govern these laws. These universal laws are systematic, predictable, unchangeable, and above all, understandable, and they were set in place by the Great Creator of the universe for our good. The Great Creator is not sitting out somewhere in the great blue yonder governing our daily application of these laws; we are, because that is our job. The Great Creator has placed the laws in operation on earth for us and to be used by us. As we travel along the pathway of this thing called life, we experience either positive consequences or negative consequences depending on whether we operate in concert with these universal laws or contrary to these universal laws.

Numerous authors have published many great works on the universal laws, albeit they are called by other names. However, these works are mere derivatives of the universal laws that were originated and placed in the universe by the Great Creator Himself. I encourage you to conduct your own study on the universal laws, and you too will find this truth to be self-evident.

During my study of the universal laws, I had occasion to read about some people's comments that the universal laws do not work for them. I have come to the conclusion that those individuals have not fully understood and embraced the full intent and application of these laws. In order for you to achieve ultimate success in your life, it is important that you align your life with these laws and principles. These universal laws and principles already exist and are waiting for you to plug into them as if you are connecting to an electrical outlet. These laws govern everything about our existence. They govern our success, wealth creation, well-being, wisdom, joy, work-life balance, and relationships. It is important that you understand the rules of the game if you want to achieve ultimate success. The first rule of the game is to understand that these universal laws and principles are biblically based whether you accept it or not. You may choose to either live in harmony with these laws, or you may choose to disregard or ignore them; the choice is yours to make. Whether you accept these laws or not, whether you admit they exist or not, or whether you believe this or not, it does not make these laws any less true.

When You Choose a Path to Success, the Universe Will Move toward You

When you set your life to agree with these universal laws and begin to operate with them and not contrary to them, you will begin to experience miraculously positive changes and great success in your circumstances. The Great Creator built the entire world on the principle of these universal laws of success, and He created you to operate successfully within them. You do not need to be a psychic to predict your future when you operate in concert with these laws. These laws are systematic, reliable, and consistent. They will work every time for everyone. These laws work whether you believe in them or not, whether you profess to be a believer or not; none of this matter. We cannot see, touch, or feel these universal laws, but we can live through them, inasmuch as we are all subject to them. What does matter is you understand and operate in agreement with these laws in order that they may work with you and for you to produce great success and abundance in your life.

As I began to focus on turning my life around and focused on achieving success, I studied the lives of many successful people. What became crystal clear to me was that most successful people operate in unison with these universal laws of success. What also became clear to me was that most unsuccessful people do not operate in unison with these laws. Perhaps either they do not know about these universal laws, or they operate contrary to these laws. The most fascinating thing about these laws is they work the same way for everyone, young, old, White, Black, Asian, American Indian, Hispanic, multiracial, male, female, disabled, or any other characteristics. These laws are unchangeable and immutable; you can predict their outcome based solely on what the Great Creator has plainly set in operation.

This book is not a study session on the universal laws; thus, I will not attempt to present all of these laws to you here. However, I strongly recommend that you conduct further study of these laws on your own. As I mentioned earlier, there are numerous authors who have devoted a significant amount of study on the universal laws, and countless books have been published on this subject.

What I will mention are those universal laws that have profoundly impacted my life. You too can experience a more satisfying and fulfilled life if you commit to learning, comprehending, cooperating with, and applying these laws in your everyday life. Each one of us has the power within us to change the conditions of our lives. We can change what we feel, what we believe, what we attract, and what we become by understanding the universal laws of success and applying the principles in such a way as to effect positive change within us and around us.

THE UNIVERSAL LAWS OF SUCCESS THAT WORKED FOR ME

The Law of A.S.K.: The Real Law of Attraction

Align your life to live in accordance with the law of A.S.K. The law of A.S.K. is often referred to by many writers as the law of attraction. Ask is a simple three-letter word with great power and when used correctly can generate great positive changes in your life. The Great Creator gave us these principles by which to receive the life we desire. In search of my true north, my journey was significantly strengthened by Matthew 7:7-8, *"Ask, and it shall be given you; seek, and ye shall find; knock, and it shall be opened unto you: For every one that asketh receiveth; and he that seeketh findeth; and to him that knocketh it shall be opened."* This entire process spells out the word *A.S.K.* and supports the analysis of the principles behind the law of attraction. To ask for something or to make a clear request is considered by far the most effective means by which we receive what we desire. What did we know about the power of A.S.K. when we were a child that we forgot when we became an adult? Even children understand the simple element of ask; it is the art of persistence. They know to keep at it until the thing they asked for is manifested in their life.

The law of A.S.K. consists of three fundamental principles, each principle is results driven even when operating singularly, but when all three principles are put into action, precept upon precept, the results are extraordinary. As we live out our daily lives, we generally operate under the principles of A.S.K., albeit many people may refer to this as living in harmony with the law of attraction, which is merely a derivative of the law of A.S.K. The blindness for most of us is that we do not realize or recognize how powerful A.S.K. is to our daily living. Because most people are unaware of the Law of A.S.K., they fail to utilize it in a conscious, deliberate, and positive method in order to accomplish their personal and professional goals. Through the process of A.S.K., you create either positive or negative thoughts, visualizations, and emotions that propel and draw you toward that which you are thinking about and hoping for. The truth of the matter is we all get what we A.S.K. for.

Apply the principles of A.S.K. until you receive, Seek until you find, and Knock until an open door appears. You can attract into your life more of what you want and eliminate that which you do not want. Through the law of A.S.K., you can create and generate energy around you that will steer you toward your path for achieving success. You become more conscious about what you want; your feelings are energized and engaged to the degree that you may actually experience psychological and behavioral changes. The key is to keep your focus on what you want without wavering or becoming engaged in other things that may be contrary to what you want, thereby negating what you desire. As you proceed under the law of A.S.K., do so with confidence and without doubt. The Great Creator also cautions against wavering thoughts. *"But let him ask in faith, with no doubting, for the one who doubts is like a wave of the sea that is driven and tossed by the wind. For that person must not suppose that he will receive anything from the Lord; a double minded man is unstable in all his ways"* (James 1:6-8). When you are unsure, doubts set in, and where there is doubt, there is confusion and uncertainty that can result into inaction, and there your dreams and hopes are stifled or dies.

Every positive or negative event that happens to us is generally the result of what we have brought into our pathway through the process of A.S.K. Be careful what you think about, ask for, and seek. As you operate in the process of Ask, Seek, and Knock, you are continually thinking and generating vibrations and sending out signals around your thinking. Through the process of optimistic thinking about what you want, positive vibrations are generated internally even before you set into motion the actions of asking, seeking, and knocking. The same is true for negative thinking. Through the process of thinking about and asking for what you want, you speak into existence various opportunities for you to receive that which you ask for and desire most, even when you do not agree that it was your own actions that generated the results you are getting.

You should believe you already have what you ask for at the time you ask for it. Although it may take time for your asking to manifest, the Great Creator has already established the principles to make manifest your thoughts. According to Mark 11:24-25, *"Therefore I tell you, whatever you ask for in prayer, believe that you have received it, and it will be yours."* When you ask for what you want, it is important for you to visualize it, see yourself with it. Through the process of visualization, go ahead and experience how it feels to receive what you desire. Hold on to that positive energy and feel the internal vibrations as you experience the visualization of what you want for your life. "As above, so below, as within, so without, as the universe, so the soul" (Hermes Trismegistus). Do not allow negative thoughts to interrupt this positive flow of energy. Dispel any negative thought patterns that try to convince you that you are unworthy and that you cannot possibly have what you are Asking, Seeking, and Knocking for. "*Fix your thoughts on what is true, honorable, and right, and pure, whatever is lovely, whatever is admirable—if anything is excellent or praiseworthy—think about such things*" (Philippians 4:8). This passage confirms that your thoughts help to create and shape your destiny. It is within your own ability to choose your thoughts. We are transformed by our thoughts as we become what we think about all day long. As you proceed through this process, the universe creates shifts (positive changes and movements) along your pathway of life steering you toward what you desire. Asking, Seeking, and Knocking are action verbs that are results driven; A.S.K. is not a passive process. Therefore, it is required that you put action behind your thoughts, or they will die in your mind.

Personal Individual Action

Set aside some time and reflect on how you can align your life with the law of ASK. Jot down your thoughts.

The Law of Sowing and Reaping

Align your life to live in accordance with the law of sowing and reaping. Some people may refer to this law as the law of cause and effect, which states that for every action there is an equal and opposite reaction. Another foundational scripture that strengthened my success journey is found in Galatians 6:7-8, "*Do not be deceived, God is not mocked; for whatever a man sows, this he will also reap.*" Although some writers may express this phenomenon as the law of cause and effect, for me it is simply you reap what you sow, you get back what you put out. If you don't like the effects of your life, you need only to stop producing the causes that are generating the unde-sired effects or results. Every action gets a reaction. As the daughter of a farmer, I have a pretty good grasp of the principles of sowing and reaping as every farmer understands the principles of seedtime and harvest time. There is a time of planting and a time to harvest what has been planted. Whatever is planted in the earth is surely returned, barring some type of natural disaster. To sustain our fam-ily, we farmed cotton, corn, cucumbers, and okra, and season after season what my father planted was returned to us in an abundance that was so plentiful that the resources sustained the family from one year to the next.

The crops always produced after their own kind and more abundantly than the seed stocks that were planted. And so it is with life—you reap what you sow, you reap in the areas of where you sow, you reap more than you sow, and you reap later and longer than you sowed. Depending on how we have lived and what we have planted, some of us may need to pray for a crop catastrophe. Whatever you plant and nourish in your heart and in your life will surely be returned to you pressed down, shaken together, and running over, as the scripture teaches.

As you live life socializing and interacting with others, you are planting seeds continuously. The types of seeds you plant are contin-gent upon you. The law of sowing and reaping works regardless of the types of seeds you plant, whether good or bad. On the positive side, these seeds could be love, fiscal resources, kindness, charity, or on the negative side, hate, destruction, or lies; it does not matter. The soil has no preference regarding the types of seed you plant in it; it just simply will multiply your seed and return to you the seeds you planted. If you want honor in your life, sow honor. If you want love in your life, sow love. If you want influence in your life, be a force multiplier by positively investing in the lives of others.

My challenge to you is that you assess your life and take an accounting of what life is producing. If you do not like what you are getting, change it. Everything that is happening in your life is a chain reaction based on the law of sowing and reaping. Don't like what you are reaping? Change what you are sowing. If you want more friendships, give more friendship. If you want to be financially independent, plant those things in your life aimed at producing wealth, such as improving your marketability for a better-paying job, start your own business, invest in wealth-producing options. Make wise investments and save more of your financial resources. If you want a promotion or a position of greater leadership and authority, invest in leadership training and educational opportunities aimed at your goal, volunteer to take on difficult assignments that highlight your skills and abilities, mentor others, and even relocate if necessary. What I am simply saying is that life will return to you what you invest in it. As you start out on this adventure of asking, seeking, and knocking, be reminded of the law of sowing and reaping. Begin to—on purpose—sow those things in your life that you want more of.

Personal Individual Action

Set aside some time and reflect on how you can align your life with the law of sowing and reaping. Jot down your thoughts.

The Law of Expectancy

Align your life to live in accordance with the law of expectancy. Live your life every day expecting great and wonderful things to happen to you and for you. Some authors refer to the law of expectancy as the self-fulfilling prophecy that says what you think you are, you are. As I took an accounting of my life, I had to overcome a poverty mentality. You know, the mind-set that mentally beats you down and whispers little lies to you such as, "You can never achieve that. Don't worry about that because it is just too hard. Some things are just not meant to be," and of course the old "good enough is good enough" attitude. To change this way of thinking and begin to live a life of expectancy, another foundational scripture I relied on for my success journey is found in Matthew 17:20, *"If ye have faith as a grain of mustard seed, ye shall say unto this mountain, 'Remove hence to yonder place;' and it shall remove; and nothing shall be impossible for you."* As you set your life to expect better and to expect great and wonderful things to happen, you will begin to see opportunities that you did not see before. We get from life what we expect to receive. I created my own formula to help me stay focused on this law: **expectancy** multiplied by **faith, confidence,** and **action** equals **positive results** (formula: E (F × C × A) = PR).

When you expect good things to happen and you put an equal amount of faith, confidence, and action behind that expectation, good things generally will happen to you and for you. The reverse can also be true; if you spend an inordinate amount of time in self-doubt and foreboding, you will get the results from that negative thinking. If you believe you can overcome obstacles and achieve success, you can, but the flip side of that coin is that if you think you can't overcome obstacles and achieve success, you generally won't. Your attitude, confidence, excitement, and the level of effort you are willing to expend on particular tasks or challenges will significantly impact the results you experience. If you think a thing is too hard for you to succeed at it, you will find failure patiently sitting and waiting around the corner for you. Change your expectations and change your results. Believing in yourself, believing in your abilities to achieve success, and getting rid of self-doubt are key components to living a life of expectancy. Expect that you can and will succeed, and you will find that you can and will succeed. Success will take persistent effort, it will take drive, it will take motivation, and there will be some difficult challenges to overcome. There will be some mountaintop experiences, and there will be some valley experiences, but if you embrace this concept of living in expectancy and allow it to influence your decisions on a daily basis, you will move mountains, and you will find that your ideal level of success is possible for you to accomplish.

Personal Individual Action

Set aside some time and reflect on how you can align your life with the law of expectancy. Jot down your thoughts.

The Law of Transformation

Align your life with the law of transformation. The Great Creator has taught us to be transformed by the renewing of our mind. Change what you are thinking about, and you can change your life. This law is BIG. Coming from the background in my life, I realized that in order to achieve a different type of life, I needed to change many preconceived patterns in my life by changing what I was thinking about. Unless I transformed my thinking, I knew that I would never raise my standard of living to the highest level possible. Another foundational scripture that I relied on as I set out on my success journey was Romans 12:2, "*Do not conform to the pattern of this world, but be transformed by the renewing of your mind.*" Often, if we are not careful, our own limiting beliefs, thoughts, and actions will hamper our own growth. It is also our own beliefs, thoughts, and actions that create vast opportunities for success.

We are limited by our own perceptions and perspectives. It is up to you to break down those mental barriers that are keeping you trapped and convincing you that you can't accomplish greatness. Understanding the law of transformation and allowing it to transform your thoughts and feelings can be a life-altering experience. Change your thinking, along with your actions, and you will transform your entire life. Let me warn you: renewing your mind to a new way of thinking and processing information differently will not be an easy evolution. You may find it somewhat difficult to change old thought processes and old patterns of living, especially when they have been a part of your life for so long. The renewing of your mind will require intentional on-purpose efforts, along with focused energy. You do not have to continue to be stuck where you are in life. You do not have to conform to your circumstances; you can change them by renewing your mind.

To begin this process, you need to see things differently. If your surroundings will not allow you to envision a different world that offers you new and exciting opportunities, you may need to travel outside of your home or your community. For example, I have an assignment for you; this is one of the things that worked for me. To see what is possible for you, you may want to find a well-appointed and pleasant hotel or some other establishment with beautiful and exquisite surroundings with great ambience. Take a pad and pen with you for jotting down notes. If you can afford it, have breakfast, lunch, and/or dinner there. Take time to soak in the beautiful surroundings and allow yourself to dream of the possibilities for your life. See yourself in a different lifestyle and living the life you deserve to have. If you do not care to have a meal at the establishment, find a quiet place to just sit and observe. Observe the people who appear as though they belong in those surroundings. Notice their traits of success. Notice their swag and the way they enter the place. Notice the way they engage and socialize with the staff and the other patrons. Notice the way they exit the establishment. Notice their walk, how they stride with confidence. They know that they belong there in a place like this. Allow your imagination to wonder, and wonder what did they do to accomplish the level of success that they now enjoy.

Whatever place you choose to help you change your focus, your vision, your thinking, and what you are dreaming about, visit it often until you get it deeply rooted in your spirit that you can indeed change the circumstances of your life to achieve the level of success you desire by renewing your mind. Visiting and experiencing a new environment that emulates what you want and desire for your life will help you in the process of renewing your mind. Your mind will respond to the mental images generated from being in a prosperous environment. Putting yourself into beautiful and prosperous surroundings will allow you to literally see the possibilities for you to obtain the level of success you are seeking. This process allows you to redirect your thinking and your thought processes toward the new possibilities that can be available in your life. This will prompt you to begin to make different and better choices. For example, when I planned our family reunions, I always made arrangements for the family to stay at fabulous hotels in order to place us in environments that were not available to us in our daily lives. This was done on purpose to expose the generation following after us to new hopes and possibilities of the life they deserved to live.

The transformation of your thoughts and actions will result through exposing yourself to new and better experiences. I can't begin to tell you how many hotel lobbies and restaurants I have sat in just observing people and the surroundings. I can't tell you how many times I left my surroundings to drive through the neighborhoods of the well-to-do and wondering, "How did they get here? What did these people do to obtain such beautiful lifestyles?" I knew that I wanted a similar lifestyle.

Change What You Say and Change the Image of Your Life

Only you can set your life in a position to achieve extraordinary success. No one can do this for you. You must assume this responsibility for yourself. If you are sincere about making changes in your life, you must change what you say about your life. No matter where you are right now in your current situation, your life can be transformed by changing what you say. Remember, Romans 12:2 states, *"Do not conform to the pattern of this world, but be transformed by the renewing of your mind."* This passage teaches us not to capitulate to unacceptable thoughts and negative things that either you have said about yourself or that you have heard others say about you. You must transform your self-speak. I challenge you to expect something different; your life will be transformed when you change your expectations by speaking positive affirmations over your life. If you truly want to live a better life, you have the innate ability to influence a better life by changing your perceptions, your expectations, your beliefs about yourself, and your abilities and by changing your self-speak.

Personal Individual Action

Set aside some time and reflect on how you can align your life with the law of transformation. Jot down your thoughts.

The Law of Increase

Align your life to live in accordance with the law of increase. Setting your life to line up with your purpose will bring increase, not only for you, but for your family as well. The Great Creator of the universe has already given us the answer of how to get increase and keep increase. Some writers refer to the law of increase as the law of reciprocity, such as "You scratch my back and I'll scratch yours." More commonly expressed as if someone gives you something, you feel an obligation to give something back to them. What became my foundation in this area was understanding the concepts behind Psalm 115:14, *"May the Lord give you increase, you and your children."* This is not as much about tangible materialistic gains, but more about the ability to obtain and retain the wisdom, understanding, and knowledge about how to continually, repeatedly, over and over again have increase in both the tangible and intangible things of life and to teach that wisdom and the application of that wisdom to the generation following after you. While it is true that applying and living in accordance with this passage will indeed produce material increase in your life, this scripture itself is more about your inner desires as connected with your purpose. When you connect with this inner purpose and operate in it, it will assist you as much in your career and professional choices as in your personal choices. All these things working together will help produce a successful and comfortable lifestyle for you and your family that meets your expectations, to include your financial expectations. I believe the correct application of Psalm 115:14, *"May the Lord give you increase, you and your children,"* is accomplished when your natural and spiritual needs are abundantly met.

What I have learned is that there are a number of applications to living a life of prosperity and abundance. For example, there is the principle of giving and receiving at work in the law of increase. Giving is a powerful energy that holds the entire universe together, and if you want to live a life of prosperity, you cannot ignore this principle. When you live by the principles of investing in the lives of others, using your resources, time, and talents, it will be returned to you in numerous different ways and more abundantly than you gave out. You can never outgive the Creator's principle of giving. Living a life as a giver played a profound role in turning my life from a life of need to a life of harmony and abundance. My true north for this way of life is found in Luke 6:38, "*Give, and it will be given to you. A good measure, pressed down, shaken together and running over, will be poured into your lap.*"

Tithing is an imperative to achieving a life of success. Through the systematic, continuous process of tithing our time, talents, and resources, we give back to the universe through linking our resources together. Through this network, lives are changed, people are fed and clothed, and communities and societies are held together for the betterment of mankind. When you tithe, you become part of that powerful successful network, and as you participate in this process of systematic giving, success will always be returned back to you in one form or another.

Charitable giving is also an imperative to achieving a life of success. Long before I had resources to give, I made it a point to give back to society such as through volunteer work. You simply must practice giving. Some examples may include financial resources, clothing, household goods, or through volunteer efforts. If you have not done so, make it a practice to begin to include those in need in your giving. One very important thing I learned to do as I set my life in alignment with giving was to ensure my pay was continuously blessed through automatic giving. I accomplished this by setting up charitable giving through payroll deductions. Do good by helping to improve the lives of others, especially those most in need, in order to effect positive change in their life and in yours as well. There are numerous ways to accomplish this, volunteering, giving to charities, supporting your local place of worship, schools, etc. Through this process, I learned to invest in the lives of others by giving back and, in many cases, by paying it forward.

Reciprocal giving is also an imperative to achieving success, more commonly known as the law of compensation. As I stated earlier, Luke 6:38, "*Give, and it will be given to you. A good measure, pressed down, shaken together and running over, will be poured into your lap.*" What you give as random acts of kindness will be returned to you. The Creator teaches that it is better to give than to receive. When you give, the universe works in a mutual beneficial way to set in process various avenues for your acts of kindness to be repaid in various different ways. We have been taught from childhood to "*do unto others as you would have them do unto you.*" It has been proven over and over again that the more you give away, the more will be returned back to you and in multiple ways. Sometimes the giving will not only be returned to you, but it will be returned to your loved ones through many generations. The Creator of the universe will use you and me as instruments of his miracle-working power in the lives of others if we will allow Him to do so. Inhabit where you live by making your home, your community, your place of worship, and your environment better. Through this process, I learned to care and invest my time, energy, and resources in where I live, where I work, and where I worship. My mother taught me that my surroundings should be better simply because I am there.

Personal Individual Action

Set aside some time and reflect on how you can align your life with the law of increase. Jot down your thoughts.

The Law of Wisdom

Align your life to seek wisdom every day! Not enough can be said about getting wisdom and understanding about a situation. Wisdom is the ability to seek out knowledge, to gain an understanding, and to correctly judge a matter. Wisdom enables you to correctly assess a situation and apply new ideals and creative solutions to deal with existing problems. I developed my success path around the foundational scripture found in Proverbs 4:5-8, "*Get wisdom, get understanding: forget it not; neither decline from the words of my mouth. Forsake her not, and she shall preserve thee: love her, and she shall keep thee. Wisdom is the principal thing; therefore, get wisdom: and with all thy getting get understanding.*" The correct application of wisdom in a matter also means considering the consequences of our actions and words and the impact they have on others. Before you act or speak, think. Wisdom also means exercising prudence by using good judgment in practical matters and relying on it to choose correctly in a given situation. A healthy reliance on wisdom will guide you in all practical matters to include employment, relationships, child-rearing, career choices, and so on. If you are seeking prosperity in your life, wisdom is the key. Wisdom is the ability to use the universal laws of success to meet and exceed your natural, spiritual, and professional expectations. It is the key that will lead you out of mediocrity into the knowledge of multiple possibilities for improving your level of success.

Personal Individual Action

Set aside some time and reflect on how you can align your life with the law of wisdom. Jot down your thoughts.

ACTION GOAL

In your journal, record the following things you can do that will align your life with the universal laws of success.

- List one or more things you can start doing that will align your life with the law of ASK.
- List one or more things you can start doing that will align your life with the law of sowing and reaping.
- List one or more things you can start doing that will align your life with the law of expectancy.
- List one or more things you can start doing that will align your life with the law of transformation.

- List one or more things you can start doing that will align your life with the law of increase.
- List one or more things you can start doing that will align your life with the law of wisdom.

Where does aligning your life with the universal laws of success fit within your personal self-assessment (personal, academic, career, financial, and/or giving aspirations)?

Part Four: Askers, Seekers, and Knockers Are Committed

- Askers, Seekers, and Knockers Exercise Dedicated Persistence and Perseverance
- Askers, Seekers, and Knockers Recognize that Choices Have Consequences
- Askers, Seekers, and Knockers Are Goal Oriented
- Askers, Seekers, and Knockers Understand that the Accomplishment of One Goal is the Beginning of a New Goal
- Askers, Seekers, and Knockers Develop and keep Good Habits

Askers, Seekers, and Knockers Exercise Dedicated Persistence and Perseverance

> Many of life's failures are people who did not realize how close they were to success when they gave up.
>
> —Thomas Edison

Achieving and maintaining a successful life takes dedicated persistence and perseverance. Growing up on a farm taught me many life lessons; among them I would rate the top two as persistence and perseverance, or more simply put, the ability to continually overcome obstacles until you achieve success as you define what that success means to you. According to *Merriam-Webster's Dictionary*, _persistence_ is defined as "continuing to do something or to try to do something even though it is difficult or other people want you to stop; continuing beyond the usual, expected, or normal time, not stopping or going away; refusing to give up or let go." _Perseverance,_ on the other hand is defined as "the quality that allows someone to continue trying to do something even though it is difficult; continued effort to do or achieve something despite difficulties, failure, or opposition." Perhaps you could say that people who exhibit the characteristics of persistence and perseverance are obsessed with accomplishing their designated goals and objectives. They accept that there can be no success without a commitment to remain persistent and the commitment to persevere no matter how many times they get knocked down; they keep getting up time after time after time because they realize that failure is not an option. They have already assessed that the cost of failure is too great, not only for them individually, but for those whose lives they touch on a daily basis. It is this type of tenacious attitude that you need if you are to overcome barriers and obstacles that are sure to present themselves along your pathway to achieving and living your life of success.

People who operate with dedicated persistence and perseverance know that victory awaits their efforts. They have identified what they want, and they go after it full force. On your road to success you cannot turn back, you cannot compromise, and you cannot quit. You must stay focused on your goals. You already have the ability to make tough choices and decision every day; you only need the willingness to act accordingly. Your dedicated persistence and perseverance will ultimately determine your commitment to success. These characteristics must be consistently operating in your life in order to live and accomplish your successful life. There is no success without hard, dedicated effort.

STORY TIME
MY STORY: Deciding to Get a College Education,
a Major Step on My Success Journey

When I decided to attend college, I was going through a divorce, living as a single parent, and working a full-time job and sometimes both a full-time and part-time jobs. The only option available for me for getting a college education was to attend classes at night and on weekends. It was unbelievably difficult, but failure was not an option. There were many, many times that I did not have a babysitter. I did not let that stop me. I took my daughter to classes with me. I put her in a chair beside me, gave her a book, a pencil, and paper, and we sat together in class. After working all day, I went to evening class and stayed up until the wee hours of the morning doing homework and studying for exams. Without a doubt, I knew that a good education would liberate me from a life of mediocrity and open doors of great opportunities. I am not ashamed to tell you that there were many times that I cried, moaned, and complained from sheer exhaustion from the struggle and the effort it took to continue on this journey.

I remember once when I was about twenty-seven years of age, I was sitting in the office of one of my college professors, having a pity party and nurturing my state of drudgery. I made the statement, "This is so hard and taking so long. When I graduate from college, I will be thirty years old." She snapped back at me, "Young lady, I suppose you will be thirty years old anyway, won't you? The difference is you will be thirty years old with a college degree." Boy, did she jerk be back into reality. I tell everyone it took me approximately six years to get a four-year degree as I did not have the luxury of going to school full-time. However, through continued dedicated persistence and perseverance, and a lot of prayers, and by taking classes at night, on weekends, and during the summer, I successfully received my bachelor of arts degree, graduating with the honors (magna cum laude). My education did not stop there. Since then I have gone on to obtain a master of arts degree, graduating with academic honors. During my career with, the federal government, I completed numerous training and development programs; however, two of the toughest and most challenging, yet the most rewarding, were successfully graduating from the US Army Management Staff College, Leadership and Development Program and successfully completing the Senior Executive Service Candidate Development Program, all of which have changed, enhanced, and improved my life in significant ways.

Throughout my life, whether it was pursuing academic degrees or pursuing a career in both the public and private sectors, I have worked hard, sought wisdom, and prayed much to accomplish my objectives. For the majority of us, a better life is not easily attained, but it is available if we are committed, dedicated, persistent, and willing to persevere and believe the unbelievable is achievable. The important lesson to take away from this section is that challenges will always present themselves in your path. The question is, what choices will you make to overcome those challenges in order to take possession of the life you deserve?

Personal Individual Action: Empowering Yourself to Achieve Greatness

Set aside some time to reflect and meditate on a point in time when you achieved a certain level of extraordinary success you desired in a particular situation even though there were many odds against your success, when against all odds you made something happen that no one believed you could do. What do you propose would happen if you exerted that level of dedicated persistence and perseverance in overcoming the challenges and obstacles you are facing today that are getting in your way of living a life of financial independence and experiencing extraordinary success in every area of your life?

ACTION GOAL

List the characteristics that you displayed in your dedication, persistence, and perseverance during this time of great effort.

Where do dedication, persistence, and perseverance fit within your personal self-assessment (personal, academic, career, financial, and/or giving aspirations)?

Askers, Seekers, and Knockers Recognize that Choices Have Consequences

> Choices are long lasting and life changing.
>
> —Reverend Diana P Cherry

Every individual is endowed with the precious gift of choice. The ability to choose has been with man since the beginning of time. That means you have the freedom to choose the path for your life; what will it be? You should not abuse this gift by living vicariously and making frequent willy-nilly decisions. We all make choices every day, and with the freedom of choice, you must exercise responsibility, wisdom, and understanding in the things you do, the things you say, and the actions you take, inasmuch as all of these things are influenced by the choices we make. Many of the choices we make are made with deliberate thought, but some are made based on unconscious rote memory. It is important to remember that every choice you make brings with it a consequence; these consequences may be good or bad, large or small, consequential or inconsequential. Nevertheless, a result follows every choice. While no one has cornered the market on how to make great choices every day, all of us have within us the ability to give careful thought to the choices we make. You have the ability to consider the circumstances you are faced with and to carefully consider the resulting consequences of your actions and then to choose the best possible course of action based on the information available to you at that particular point in time.

All of us are guilty of the worst fate of having made, at some point in time, some terrible choices and having suffered the consequences of those choices. There are probably times when you may have allowed other people to influence your choices, and what seemed like a great idea at that time turned out to be a huge mistake that you came to regret. There is no doubt that as long as we live we will again make some unwise choices, but that does not have to be a way of life for any of us. On the other hand, I will bet that you have made some great and fantastic choices that have led to great results in your life. Right now today, you have the freedom to make your own choices, but at the same time, you must be willing to accept full responsibility for the choices that you make. Your decisions may not only affect your life, but the lives of others that you have responsibility for. For that reason, it is important that you exercise good decision-making skills in your everyday life.

You and I both know people who are too willing to shift the blame to others for their own poor choices. People want to blame their parents, the economy, society, the court system, their bosses, discrimination, the school system, or whomever or whatever is available to blame. The truth of the matter is, ultimately each individual is responsible for the situation and conditions of their own life. Accepting responsibility for your actions and for the choices that you make is an important step to living a successful life. When you are faced with the challenge of making a valued choice, you should consider your choices carefully, seek wise counsel, weigh the consequences of your options, use forethought, and be sure you have a good understanding of the situation before you. Never ever be influenced by immoral factors in your decision-making. Your decisions should align with your values systems and your priorities. It may take a good amount of intestinal fortitude to make a tough decision, but you will find that your life and the lives of those whom you influence will be better off when you stand firmly for what is right and just. Remember, while you have the freedom to make the choice, you do not have the ability to control the impact or the consequences of your choices as experienced by others.

Askers, Seekers, and Knockers get fired up about making choices, taking responsibility for their life and holding themselves accountable for their success and/or their failures. They repeatedly question themselves about their life, such as, "What do I want my life to be? When do I want this for my life? And why is my life where it is?" They also realize that there is a price to be paid, so they count the cost of doing and not doing the what, when, how, and why of their life choices. Askers, Seekers, and Knockers are those who train their natural mind to listen to their inner spirit. You must train your inner spirit to ask questions about your natural circumstances. You must develop your inner spirit to respond by guiding natural human choices in the direction of a positive life with positive influence. From a natural human perspective, we have not always been taught to develop our spirituality by listening to and developing our inner spirit. Starting now, you must understand that while we are made up of physical matter, which makes us human beings, we are at the same time spiritual beings having natural experiences. Therefore, our spirit oftentimes goes undeveloped. Our spirit is a very powerful part of who we are, and it can have great influence in guiding and leading us through the wisdom of choice, if we allow it to be so.

A time may present itself where you are facing a situation where you feel pressured to make a life-changing decision impulsively. I will caution that this is not the best time to make a values-based decision. Many poor decisions have been made under pressure and during times of chaos and stress. If you should find yourself in this type of situation, try taking a moment to step back from the situation and connect with your spirit. Ask your spirit to lead you through wisdom. Find a place of respite and take the necessary time to evaluate the situation and the options before you.

One of the greatest freedoms you will ever possess is your freedom of choice. What you do every day is what you choose to do; what is missing from your life is what you choose not to do or not to have. You always have a choice, and no one can take that away from you. You are in control of your own thoughts and choices. Making better choices every day makes us better people. Your choices will ultimately control your destiny, your level of financial independence, where you live, work, and play, and whether you live and extraordinarily successful life—or NOT.

Personal Individual Action: Controlling Your Destiny through Choices

Set aside some time to reflect and meditate on some of the major life choices you made that landed you in a particularly good place in life and those that landed you in a particularly challenging place in life. Did you experience any aha moments?

ACTION GOAL

Record those things that were going on in your life that drove you to make the choices you made. Identify valuable life lessons you learned that you will keep in your life and those you will release from your life.

Where does the ability to choose wisely fit within your personal self-assessment (personal, academic, career, financial, and/or giving aspirations)?

Askers, Seekers, and Knockers Are Goal Oriented

> Goal Setting is the First Step to turning the Invisible into the Visible.
> —Tony Robins

Goal setting is one of the first steps toward believing what you once thought was unbelievable for you and achieving what you once believed was impossible for you to achieve. If you are tired of working hard, spinning your wheels and feeling as though you are getting nowhere in life, try setting specific goals with clearly defined objectives and timelines. Never ever allow anyone to convince you that setting goals are unimportant. Do not allow anyone to convince you that writing and prioritizing goals are equally unimportant. Goal setting is where you take real responsibility for your own success. I also recommend that you get yourself an accountability partner to help hold you accountable for sticking to your goals.

Establishing and writing your goals is a powerful process that will help you clarify what you want out of life. This process will also help you design a road map for your new journey to success that will get you from where you are today to where you want to be tomorrow. Goal setting will also help you identity your journey, the important paths you should embark upon, how to prepare for the journey, how long the journey will take, and your progress along the way. Setting goals will also help you identify what obstacles may be preventing you from completing your journey. This will help you identify what resources are required for accomplishing your goals and how to go after those resources. Most important, goal setting will equip you with the ability to identify your end goal when you have reached your destination. At the end of each goal accomplishment, create a space for celebrating the achievement of your goal. Goal setting forces you to take responsibility for the success you want to achieve as opposed to sitting around and accepting what life throws at you. When you set goals for your life, you chart your own path, and you make your own decisions rather than you becoming a Mephibosheth by letting other people make those decisions for you.

As I studied the lives and patterns of many successful people, the one thing I found that was vehemently clear in these people's success stories is that they had specific, measurable, achievable, and realistic results-driven goals. They identified where they were, where they wanted to be, and what it would take to get them from where they were to where they wanted to be. Further, they made their own decisions about their life. While you may find that goal setting and accomplishments are not easy tasks to manage and can sometimes even seem overwhelming, this should not be a reason for not taking on these challenges. The important thing is to not become discouraged because you run into disappointments and setbacks. This is life, and in life there will always be successes combined with failures and disappointments on any journey you decide to take. But there will also be great joy and satisfaction that will eventually outweigh the setbacks.

Your Goals Should Be Written

When you get serious about achieving and living a successful life, you will not only set goals for your life; you will design specific goals, and you will put them in writing where they can be reviewed and acted upon on a daily basis. Write the vision and make it plain; this will help you set right the vision for your life. Until you are actually ready to commit your goals to writing, you are simply in a state of perpetual reverie (continuous daydreaming) about what you want out of life. Putting your goals in writing will force you to stop procrastinating and take specific actions. It's time to get the dream out of your head and down on paper. Written goals bring visibility and focus to your desired outcomes. After you put your goals in writing, post your goals on your mirror, on the refrigerator, in your bedroom, and anywhere else where they can constantly remind you of your commitments. Create a vision board and add your goals to it.

Your Goals Should Be Specific

Your goals should have specificity. General, broad goals may serve well as goal headings, such as "I want to live a life of financial independence." From this broad goal, specific goals should then be developed as related to the different aspects of your life that will help propel you toward that goal. For instance, if you have a family, setting a broad goal to live a life of financial independence should most certainly take into account consideration of your family. If one of your goals include living on a budget and you developed certain specific objectives designed to pay off credit cards and eliminate unnecessary spending within a certain time period, this goal would certainly require the cooperation of your spouse and children. Will one of your goals include preparing yourself to obtain a new position with better pay and benefits? What about increasing the amount set aside for savings? Create simple objectives and milestones that will take you step by step to achieving your goals.

Your Goals Should Be Measurable

The goals that you develop must have measurable outcomes that represent your achievements. These outcomes are generally referred to as results. Create specific objectives to go along with your goals. These objectives should be designed to guide you along the pathway toward accomplishing your results. This is the only way you will be able to determine whether you actually have successfully accomplished what you set out do. Measurable outcomes will also enable you to track the progress of your intended results. By building in measurable results, you will be able to determine what is going right, what is not going well, and what should be corrected if necessary. But most important, measurements will allow you to be able to determine when you have successfully reached the goal when you are FINISHED!

Your Goals Should Be Achievable

Each goal should be something that you can definitely achieve even though it may be difficult to achieve. Setting goals with a certain level of difficulty designed to stretch you are ideal for growth and development. However, creating a goal that is too lofty and unrealistic to achieve will defeat your purpose for goal setting. If you set a goal simply because it sounds good yet not even you believe you can achieve it, it is doubtful that you will exert the energy to even try reaching it. Every goal should have a certain level of self-efficacy where you actually believe that the goal is valuable, useful, and you have the ability to achieve it within the time period you establish. When working toward your goals, if you find that a specific goal requires an adjustment, be willing to make course corrections where required in order to keep on track. But be cautious not to lower your goal expectations simply because you do not want to exert the required effort to achieve the goal.

Your Goals Should Have Defined Deadlines

Your goal will be of little value unless you assign it a specific timeframe to be accomplished with a specific start date and completion date. This will allow you to get prepared to take on your new journey. When setting your timeframes, consider external factors that may come up that are beyond your control. Be prepared to deal with unexpected challenges that could delay your progress. You may find it necessary to add additional checkpoints in your timeframe in order to ensure you remain on track. This will also allow you to adjust your completion dates where warranted.

Your Goals Should Have an Accountability Partner

As with any new project, it is easy to become inundated with the issues of life, and this could impact your ability to stay on track with your goals. Goal setting and living up to your goals are tough stuff; this is not child's play. Therefore, you may find it an excellent idea to solicit the support of an accountability partner. This can be a trusted friend, a family member, or a coworker who cares enough about you to want to help you succeed. Your accountability partner is someone who is willing to serve as your emotional supporter, motivator, and encourager. This is the person who is willing to inspire you and help keep you accountable and on track with your goals and objectives as you take on this new journey of seeking a successful life. The extra added incentive of knowing that you are expected to check in and give an accountability report about your progress can prove to be just the shot in the arm you need in the middle of a tough time when it is hard to keep focused. Point to remember, your accountability partner cannot be just a "yes" person. This must be someone who is willing to be brutally honest with you when you are not doing what you should be doing.

Your Goals Should Be Celebrated

Goal achievement is worth celebrating! You should definitely create a space in your life to celebrate not only the achievement of a specific goal, but for accomplishing objectives along the way. This will serve as a great motivator to help you keep on track and hang in there when the going gets tough. There is tremendous satisfaction associated with accomplishing your goals, and your achievements should definitely be tracked and celebrated. At the end of each goal, you will notice that your self-confidence will be boosted, and you will feel reinvigorated and encouraged to continue on your journey. Don't skimp on rewarding yourself for all of your hard work, and be sure to invite your accountability partner to join in the fun of the celebration. A word of caution for your celebration: don't allow the celebration to undo your accomplishments and hard work. During the celebration, pay tribute to the people who helped you and the things you did to get you to this level of success.

If you are just beginning the process of goal setting, try starting out with small goals, and after you master that objective gradually, set greater goals. For example, if you have a goal to get a promotion on your job, start out by identifying any additional training you may need and take it. Identify additional duties and responsibilities you may voluntarily take on to help improve your skills, and do them. Identify different offices or departments that offer opportunities that can assist you. Identify leaders who are able to assist you in achieving this goal and ask them to coach or mentor you. Look at possible opportunities outside of your organization, and set dates and time-lines associated with specific objectives aimed at moving you closer to your target. One thing is for certain: nothing will happen until you make a move. The ball is in your court.

STORY TIME
MY STORY: Shut That Television Off and You Can Do Something!

When I finally made the choice to shut the television off and do something about writing this book, I was able to accomplish a goal that I had planned to do for many years. I have wanted to write this book since 2006, and from 2006 until about a year ago, nothing of any real value happened in terms of writing this book. In 2008, I actually wrote about ten to twelve pages, and then from 2008 until recently, the only thing I did was talk about wanting to write this book. Finally, a few years ago, one evening after a particularly long and hard day at work, I was sitting on my sofa, watching television and having a pity party, complaining and whining to my Creator about how difficult it would be for me to write a book. My excuses ranged from my job is too difficult and complex, I work such long hours, I don't know where to begin, etc. And you know how the story goes "Woe is me," blasé this and blasé that. Suddenly, my Creator filled my entire spirit with "If you shut that television off, you can do something." Wow! I knew right away that Yeshua had no pity or patience with me and my attitude of laziness and excuses. If I was ever to write this book, I needed to do something to take control of my life. I realized that until I made a move, nothing was going to happen. The next day I put pencil to paper and developed my goals that would help move me from inaction to action.

My first set of goals were developed to steer me toward restructuring my workday so that I would leave my office within a reasonable time after my work day ended rather than staying on the job until seven and eight o'clock at night, which was well beyond my work schedule, which normally ended at 4:30 p.m. To help me adhere to this goal, I enlisted the support of my daughter to serve as my accountability partner to help me stay focused on this goal. This was a tremendous help; with her support and sometimes badgering, I left the office most days within a reasonable time, mostly no later than an hour or so past my normal work schedule.

My second set of goals focused on setting aside a set amount of time to get home, unwind, prepare dinner, and watch a small amount of television only while I prepared and ate dinner. After which, the television was immediately turned off, and downstairs to my office I went to focus on my third set of goals.

My third set of goals was developed to get me prepared for writing this book. I had absolutely no training in writing a book and did not have a clue on how to get started. As I took the initiative to do something, a friend of mine happened to send me a link to several programs that he thought might prove useful in my quest. As I took one on-line course after another, my research finally led me to a link called "Bestseller Blueprint.com". This is an on-line writing course developed by Steve Harrison of Bradley Communications and Jack Canfield, bestselling author of "Chicken Soup for the Soul" and numerous other publications. This program was the stepping-stone that catapulted me forward and set me on the path to writing this book.

The fourth set of goals was developed to guide me every day in doing something constructive to fulfill my goal of actually writing the first manuscript. These goals were the most stringent. I remember writing into my goals the requirement that I had to prepare a written justification to myself if I missed a day of doing something that moved me forward in working on the manuscript. The requirement for a written justification became my invisible accountability partner. I was often amazed at the power this requirement held over me. I found that I did not want to have to justify to myself why I had not honored my own commitment; thus, I found that I was dedicated to my goals and commitment.

I found that committing my goals to writing gave me vision, focus, direction, and a determination to succeed at all costs. Speaking of costs, I also had to come to terms with the realization that accomplishing these goals would cost me not only my time, but fiscal resources as well. I had to be willing to invest in myself in order to achieve greatness. There is a cost to be paid in almost everything worth achieving, and you must be willing to pay the cost personally and financially. This type of investment will repay you in dividends more numerous than you can imagine. And it all starts with goal setting. Make the choice today to create your goals that will change your behaviors and set you on the path to greatness in order for you to live the abundant life you were born to live. People who set goals succeed!

Personal Individual Action: Creating New Possibilities by Creating Goals

Set aside some time for reflection and meditation about where you are in life and whether you have utilized goals and objectives to get you there. It is time to start thinking about developing your goals and objectives regarding your personal, academic, career, financial, and/or giving aspirations. As you think about a goal, think in terms of a broad overarching principle that guides decision-making in that particular area of your life. The corresponding objectives are more narrowly defined specific steps designed to help you accomplish reaching your goals in that particular area of your life. As you ponder the idea of developing your goals and objectives, think about how you will measure successful accomplishment. We will refine your goals and objectives later.

ACTION GOAL

Lay out the headings of personal, academic, career, financial, and/or giving aspirations. In a very rough draft format, begin to jot down ideas of what you hope to accomplish in these areas and what it will take to achieve what you have listed. This is the beginning phase of goal development.

Where does creating goals and objectives fit within your personal self-assessment (personal, academic, career, financial, and/or giving aspirations)?

Askers, Seekers, and Knockers Understand that the Accomplishment of One Goal Is the Beginning of a New Goal

People with Goals Succeed because they know where they are going, it is as simple as that.

—Earl Nightingale

Askers, Seekers, and Knockers know that successful goal achievement and accomplishment generates new possibilities within themselves that they may once never have imagined. The accomplishment of one goal strengthens you for the next goal. Goal setting is a continuous process in the lives of successful people where they are always looking for ways to improve life for themselves and for others whom they influence. They know that the completion of each goal, no matter how small or how large, is another step forward in achieving and living an extraordinarily successful life. They take time to reflect and savor their accomplishments. With each succession of goal achievement, Askers, Seekers, and Knockers are encouraged to continue on their journey. The positive energy you gain along the way will serve as fuel to spur you on and help you climb over other challenges that present themselves along your journey. With great anticipation and excitement, Askers, Seekers, and Knockers acknowledge that the successful completion of one set of goals is no time to rest on their past laurels, but rather it is a time to begin preparing for the new journey that lies ahead of them.

As Askers, Seekers, and Knockers complete their goals and objectives, they are able to measure and document new habits and effective patterns being formed in their life. It is the development of these new habits and patterns that Askers, Seekers, and Knockers rely on for developing formulas for success. Askers, Seekers, and Knockers' success formulas keep their lives on a successful path. With each successful goal completion, Askers, Seekers, and Knockers gain new experiences and lessons learned that they use as building blocks for the next goal. These lessons guide and teach Askers, Seekers, and Knockers more and more about what it takes to achieve new goals and objectives that they may never have imagined as possibilities.

Personal Individual Action: Self-Improvement Is a Continuous Process

Set aside some time to work on refining the goals and objectives you started in the previous section.

ACTION GOAL

Spend some time studying about developing achievable goals and objectives. If you need help, you will find that there are numerous resources that can help you with writing and developing goals. However, this is not so much about what other people think as it is about what you think and what you want for your life. So get the help if you think you need it, but remember that this is about you and your desires.

Where does continuous self-improvement fit within your personal self-assessment (personal, academic, career, financial, and/or giving aspirations)?

Askers, Seekers, and Knockers Develop and Keep Good Habits

> Sow a thought, and you reap an act; Sow an act, and you reap a habit; Sow a habit, and you reap a character; Sow a character, and you reap a destiny.
>
> —Charles Reade

The importance of developing good habits cannot be overstated as you walk your journey of success. In my continued quest to study the lives of successful people, among the many important things I learned is that successful people have inculcated into their everyday lives effective habits. It is these habits, more than anything, that have positively influenced their behaviors and value systems. While setting goals is at the top of my list, I have come to realize that without the establishment of good daily habits, it will be impossible to achieve those goals. Your success will indeed depend on the quality of positive, effective habits that you develop and instill into your everyday life.

When I decided to change my life, I first had to face my truth, which was I was where I was because of my choices and because of my own poor habits. I realized these habits were getting me nowhere. As I mentioned earlier, when I decided to write this book, I first had to break several bad habits, such as spending too much time at work after my workday ended and spending too much time watching television. The success that I now enjoy is in direct proportion to the habits that I developed and gradually implemented into my life and daily schedule. Many of these habits were formed through life lessons and through my associations with numerous successful people. Throughout my studies and work life, I have had the privilege of interacting with many successful and impressive individuals, including college professors, members of the military, ministers, medical providers, members of the Senior Executive Service, law enforcement personnel, and other professionals, all of whom have left their indelible imprint on my life.

On your road to success, you will have the ability to examine the lives of numerous successful people; you too will find many commonalities in these individuals' lives that contributed to their success. You will find that most successful people share many of the same habits, and some of these habits may not be very different from your successful habits. But at the end of the day, no matter how many successful people you study, unless you are willing to do the hard work and change your own habits and implement new ones, positive change will never take place in your life. It is up to you and you alone to define and develop the habits that will lead you to great success. Listed below are the habits that I have built into my everyday life. These are my eight habits for successful living. These habits have worked extraordinarily well for me; hopefully, these will work for you too.

HABIT #1: Strive for Excellence Every Day

Never settle for mediocrity. You must strive for excellence in all of your endeavors. Many years ago, when I was promoted to my first supervisory position in the federal government, I found a quote that I framed and posted upon my wall. I have kept that quote with me since that day, and I continue to post that quote on my office wall, on the wall of my home, and on the wall of my heart. The author of the quote is unknown, but the quote reads, *"Excellence can be achieved if you risk more than others think is safe, care more than others think is wise, dream more than others think is practical, and expect more than others think is possible."* Excellence can be achieved in your daily endeavors if you make it the cornerstone of your efforts.

HABIT #2: Stay Committed until Success Is Achieved

I can't emphasize this enough: you must exercise commitment, dedication, persistence, perseverance, and hard work every day in order to overcome obstacles and reach success in any endeavor you set out to achieve. As you travel your journey of success, you will quickly realize that successful men and women encountered numerous obstacles that they had to overcome. Nevertheless, they faced these obstacles with a determination that they would succeed, and so can you.

HABIT #3: Be Goal Oriented

Set goals that will force you to grow and develop. Identify what you want and develop a plan of action to get you from where you are today to where you want to be tomorrow. Commit the plan to writing, review it every day, and do something each day that propels you toward finishing. Live every day with a mind-set of continuous improvement, recognizing that the completion of one goal is an opportunity to begin a new goal. Life is progressive; as long as there is breath in your body, you should never stop growing and reaching for the next level.

HABIT #4: Respect and Value People

Treat people with respect and believe that people are basically good and that everyone has value. When you meet an individual, assign them a value of 10 on the people scale of 1 to 10. If the number value moves anywhere below10, let that movement be based on the actions of the individual and not on your assumptions. This principle was taught to me by Ms. Lula Dickson, the first African American female at Pine Bluff Arsenal to achieve the rank of GS-13. I have always carried this principle with me, and I continue to live with it by letting it govern the way I treat and interact with people.

HABIT #5: Take Care of Yourself by Maintaining Good Health and a Balanced Lifestyle

Take care of your physical and emotional health and maintain a sense of balance in your life. Your health and well-being are the greatest of all your assets, and without either of these, your success will be limited. Take time out for renewal, grow spiritually, schedule and attend medical checkups, exercise regularly, get enough sleep, eat right, set boundaries, go on vacation, participate in recreational activities, go out to dinner and to an uplifting movie occasionally, and just say no before stretching yourself too thin.

HABIT #6: Believe in Something Bigger Than Yourself

For me, a belief in something bigger than myself is my core belief in God the Creator of the universe and His son Yeshua. It is important that you identify your core beliefs and values and take the necessary time for spiritual renewal. Get centered through acts of meditation and gratitude and by drawing upon the truth, which grounds you to your spirituality and your value systems. I regularly take time to renew my spiritual growth and development through worship, study, reflections, and meditations.

Develop a personal relationship with your spirituality. It is difficult to have a sincere and intimate relationship with someone whom you do not know or trust. The only way to do this is to spend time studying and practicing your beliefs. This is about relationship building. Through the process of study and meditation, you will learn to love, to trust, and to on purpose follow instructions, wisdom, and guidance for your life.

Study continually, have faith, trust, and believe in the faithfulness of the Great Creator's commitment and promises toward you. Through this process, I learned that as I cared and attended to His purpose, He was faithful in caring for me. The time you spend in reflections and meditation should not be forced time; it should be relaxed and enjoyable. I have learned that the inner spirit is more receptive to direction, guidance, and instructions when the spirit, mind, and body are in a relaxed state. Totally trust, believe, and have faith that the plans you make for your life will come to fruition. Discuss your plans with an accountability partner, seek guidance about them, and be willing to let your faith bring order and success in your life.

HABIT #7: Wake Up Every Day Believing You Were Created for Greatness

The revelation of your greatness first begins in your mind. You become what and who you believe you are. You are equipped with everything you need to develop a mind-set of prosperity and to create a life of extraordinary success. Nurture your dreams, your ideas, and your aspirations. You will ultimately attract into your life what you give your focus and attention to. Believe that you are a conqueror, you are courageous, you are amazing, and you are the champion of your cause.

HABIT #8: Stop Doing What Is Not Working!

I believe it was Albert Einstein who explained that the definition of *insanity* is "doing the same thing over and over again and expecting different results." Simply put, stop doing those things that are generating negative results or the results that you do not want for your life. One purpose for doing the reflection and meditation exercises is to review what is working for you and what is not working for you so that you can eliminate ineffective behaviors. I did it, and so can you.

> Your beliefs become your thoughts,
> Your thoughts become your words,
> Your words become your actions,
> Your actions become your habits,
> Your habits become your values,
> Your values become your destiny.
> **—Mahatma Gandhi**

Personal Individual Action: Getting to Greatness through a Disciplined Life

Set aside some time to reflect and meditate on your habits, the good ones and the damaging ones. Reflect on how your habits have helped you and on how your habits have hampered your success in life. Give a significant amount of thought to the habits you need to eliminate from your life, the habits you will retain for your life, and the new habits you will develop for your life. Where does discipline fit within this picture?

ACTION GOAL

This is a very important exercise. Your habits should be designed to move you from where you do not want to be to where you want to be, but this requires living a disciplined life. As you think about what you want to achieve in your new goals and objectives, create new habits (things you want to do every day) around those goals. This could be something as simple as repeating an affirmation that will help you achieve a particular goal. It may also be something as simple as "I will finish my chores and get to bed on time each night so that I am better prepared to report to work on time each day." Your habits should be designed to support your efforts to reach your goals and objectives. *Self-discipline* is the operative word in developing new successful habits.

Where does creating and keeping good habits fit within your personal self-assessment (personal, academic, career, financial, and/ or giving aspirations)?

Part Five: Askers, Seekers, and Knockers Are Unstoppable

- Askers, Seekers, and Knockers Know That They Know, That They Know, They Are Destined for Greatness
- Askers, Seekers, and Knockers Do Not See Failing as Defeat, They See Another Opportunity to Succeed
- Askers, Seekers, and Knockers Do Not Allow a Difficult Beginning in Life to Dictate their End
- Askers, Seekers, and Knockers Take Life On and Choose to be Happy—Life is Good!
- Askers, Seekers, and Knockers Know That Adversity Is a Natural Part of Living

Askers, Seekers, and Knockers Know that They Know that They Know They Are Destined for Greatness

> You were put on this earth to achieve your greatest self, to live out your purpose, and to do it courageously.
>
> —Steve Maraboli

Have you ever had a knowing deep inside of you that tells you that you are capable of so much more than what surrounds you? But you look around and you see no evidence of greatness manifested in your life. I felt this way most of my young adult life. Often, we are products of our conditioning, thoughts, and limiting belief systems. When your expectations and beliefs about your abilities and capabilities are influenced by those around you who are also held back by their limitations, your mental programming will often reflect such. It is about time for you to come to terms with the realization that you were born to do great things; you were born for such a time as this. Askers, Seekers, and Knockers know that they are destined for greatness long before they are great. You have a skill, a talent, and a purpose that the world is waiting for, but only you can produce and develop the uniqueness you possess by deciding to walk it out. Your destiny is in your hands!

Knowing that you are destined for bigger and better things but your circumstances tell you differently reminds me of the biblical story of Ester. I encourage you to read the full text on your own. This is a story of a young beautiful Jewish woman who was plunged into one of the greatest stories of all time through a series of incidents that could have cost her, her very life. These events brought Ester face-to-face with her destiny. She was born to become the queen of Persia, but you would never have known that based on the circumstances she was born into. Eventually, destiny and circumstances converged in such a way that she became a part of the king's palace. Suddenly she found herself facing a serious challenge where she would have to make a life-or-death decision. It took a great amount of courage and risk-taking. Nevertheless, she stepped into her destiny and was able to expose a plot that would have led to the destruction of her people. I encourage you to read this story as you will probably notice some important parallel points to your life. She was not born into greatness, and greatness was not around her. Life circumstances brought her to a point where a road of opportunity presented itself, and she made the choice to take that road. As she embarked upon this road of opportunity, she was required to go through an extended process of preparation before assuming her new role in the kingdom. As she walked in her destiny, she was faced with making difficult life-changing choices that would either improve her lifestyle or had the possibility of destroying her lifestyle.

You too may find yourself facing many difficulties, but just like Ester, who knows whether or not you have come to this place in your life for such a time as this? This is an excellent story, and I encourage you to read it in its entirety as the life of Ester teaches several vital lessons about accepting and walking into your destiny. Ester started out as an orphan but ended up as a queen who saved an entire generation of people. The moral of this story is that your beginning does not necessarily determine your greatness or your ending, but your choices will. Your destiny will cost you something; the choice is up to you whether you will be willing and prepared to make the sacrifices and pay the cost.

Your destiny, your personal, spiritual, academic, and professional growth are your responsibilities and yours alone. No one else is responsible for the success you will or will not achieve. There is no easy road to greatness. Just as in the life of Ester, your choices will dictate and control your destiny. Great people are great because they are willing to do what few people are willing to do, and that is the hard stuff. It is through making tough choices and facing difficult circumstances that you can transform and transcend into an individual greater than who you are now. It is your responsibility to develop the road map that will set you on your path to greatness.

Although you may feel and believe in your heart of hearts that you are destined for greatness, you will never achieve your greatness until you are willing to do the hard things by preparing yourself for the challenges that lay ahead. Your destiny will not grow legs and walk up to you; instead, you will have to walk into your destiny. You must be willing to grow and expand into the difficult areas. Never, ever allow mediocrity to find a home in your thoughts, beliefs, attitude, and actions. Mediocrity is the killer of your destiny to greatness.

You cannot allow anything to stand in your way, not your age, your disability, or any other obstacles that you may be facing. On your way to greatness, you will encounter many obstacles, but the greatest obstacle you will encounter is you and your attitude. You will become tired and weary, and you will have to fight against your fears, your doubts, and that inner quiet voice that becomes weary and whispers ever so quietly, "I am tired of this struggle. Who do you think you are? You are nobody. You can never be that great. That type of life is not for people like you. You don't deserve that." You must be willing to face yourself in the mirror and destroy the negative voices with even more powerful affirmations that strengthen your spirit with words of encouragement.

I remember once when I was going through a difficult outdoor training program called HEARTS Training. We were taught a quote that said, "*There is no growth in the comfort zone; and no comfort in the growth zone.*" That is a profound statement with significant meaning. This training is among some of the best training programs I have ever attended. It forced me to face my fears and doubts by overcoming some significant obstacles I never dreamed I could conquer. You too must develop this mind-set while on your road to greatness.

Greatness requires a total commitment if you are to achieve your dreams and aspirations.

Walking into greatness takes deliberate preparation. As I studied the lives of many great successful people, I discovered that they had numerous stories to tell of the times and struggles they went through when they were not so great and they tell story after story about the things they did and went through on their journey to greatness. It is their stories that encouraged me, and I encourage you to read the life stories about your heroes because they will encourage you too. Unfortunately, many people are not willing to pay the price and go through the sacrifices, the hard periods, and the growing pains. They want the rewards of a great and successful life right now without any suffering. But success and greatness are never achieved overnight; it takes hard work and a period of dedicated, thought-provoking preparedness. Greatness is not held in reserve for a predetermined group of people; it lies at the feet of anyone who is willing to make the sacrifices and pay the price to be great and successful. Success will always remain aloof to the wannabes who just want it, but are not willing to use their maximum potential to achieve it. No matter what you are facing in your life today and no matter what is happening around you, there is something special about you, and within you lies your greatness.

You have the ability to break down the barriers of limiting beliefs that are holding you hostage to a life of unrealized achievements. You can overcome these invisible barriers through empowering yourself to take charge of your life. It's time for you to change your thinking and take the necessary steps to equip yourself for the great journey that you are about to embark upon. This may mean returning to school, changing jobs, relocating, changing your associations, and creating and repeating positive self-affirmations about your strengths, abilities, and capabilities. It will also mean setting and accomplishing goals and creating action plans to map out your future. You were born with a great plan for your life, and you have something great to offer to your family, your community, your place of worship, your profession, and this world. There is a great journey that lies within that you were created to take. The world is waiting for you. My question is, will you take the journey?

Personal Individual Action: Wake Up—The World Is Waiting for You and Your Abilities

Set aside some time to reflect and meditate on the thoughts, ideas, concepts, and hunches that you have often had that showed you in the light of you achieving more and being more than what you see around you at the present time. This is the spiritual or subconscious desperately trying to communicate to you that you are destined for greatness.

ACTION GOAL

Give your creative imagination permission to come alive. Record (without restraint) the big thoughts, ideas, concepts, and hunches that you have imagined your life to be; you can refine your thoughts later. Go through this exercise frequently, allowing your mind to be stimulated by the possibilities of what can be. It is a well-documented fact that some of our best ideas and solutions to challenges come through taking off the constraints of a creative imagination.

Where does opening up your creative mind to new possibilities fit within your personal self-assessment (personal, academic, career, financial, and/or giving aspirations)?

Askers, Seekers, and Knockers Do Not See Failing as Defeat, They See Another Opportunity to Succeed

> The difficulties and struggles of today are but the price we must pay for the accomplishments and victories of tomorrow.
>
> —William J. H. Boetcker

Fighting for your success is not for the faint of heart who only want to play it safe. This fight is for those who may fail repeatedly, but they keep getting up repeatedly until they win. They understand that making mistakes are a natural progression toward achieving success. Everyone wants to avoid failure, but failing is inevitable, and it happens to each and every one of us from time to time. The good news is failing is not defeat, and it is neither a permanent state in your life, unless you make it permanent. Failure is merely a temporary setback that creates new experiences in your life. It is a new chance to learn, and it is one more opportunity to succeed. Failure and defeat can sometimes be your greatest teachers, because it is through making mistakes that we often learn the most. The only real failure is giving up and failing to try again.

I am often referred to as an expert in my career field, and I mentor a number of careerists in this field. One question that is often posed to me is, "Ms. McMillon, how did you become so knowledgeable about this field?" My answer is, "First, I continually study. Second, I have made many mistake in this line of work, but most important, I try not to make the same mistake twice. Instead, I use these as learning experiences. Third, I am a risk-taker. Fourth, I am not afraid of making a decision, even with limited information. And fifth, I no longer fear failing."

I have learned that an expert in his or her field is simply someone who has failed more often than most other people in the same line of work because they are not afraid to step outside of their comfort zone. That is how you grow and become an expert in your chosen profession. I will not lie to you, and you know this to be true: failing does not feel good. In fact, it feels downright awful. If you allow it, failing will create doubts, fears, and feelings of defeat, but you do not have to settle for this temporary state, and it is no reason to quit trying. With each failure, new lessons are learned that move you up one notch closer to your goal of success. Everybody will fail at something before they are great, and some people fail more often and further than others do. Accept it, you will fail and you will face defeat and you will want to do the easiest thing, which is quitting. However, if you quit, you will never know whether your goal of success was just on the other side of one more try. There is no reward to be received if you quit and choose to live in defeat. If you intend to turn your impossible into possibilities and reach your greatest potential, you must get over your fear of failing. That is the attitude taken by some of the greatest athletes, inventors, talk show hosts, authors, CEOs, and presidents the world has ever known. Listed below is a list of some of the great people whose lives and challenges I studied on my success journey. These people used their failures as stepping-stones to catapult them toward achieving great success. Just to name a few:

Jack Canfield and Mark Victor Hansen received 143 rejections for their *Chicken Soup for the Soul* book before it was published. Since that time, the book has sold over ten million copies, and Jack Canfield is now recognized as one of the world's most famous authors, motivational speakers, seminar leaders, corporate trainers, and entrepreneur.

Michael Jordan, one of the world's greatest basketball players, was cut from his high school basketball team when he was a sophomore. Since that time, he has become known as one of the world's most famous and riches basketball superstars and world-renowned athlete.

Thomas Edison failed more than a thousand times before he successfully created the light bulb. He is now recognized as one of the world's greatest historical figures for his inventions to include the central power station and the phonograph, among other things.

Albert Einstein did not speak until he was four years old and struggled with reading in his early years. Nevertheless, he developed the theory of relativity and went on to become recognized as one of the world's most influential physicist today.

Les Brown was born on the floor of an abandoned building, labeled mentally retarded, and grew up poor. Since that time, he has overcome numerous obstacles. He became a syndicated talk show host, lost the show, overcame more obstacles, and is now recognized as one of the world's most highly acclaimed and dynamic motivational speakers known to the modern world.

Steve Jobs, founder and former CEO of Apple, was fired from his own company before he returned to the company to save it from failure. He turned the company around, and you know the rest of the story about Apple. It is a world-renowned company, and you are probably using one of their many electronic devices.

Walter E. "Walt" Disney was once told he lacked imagination and vision. He failed in several business ventures and even filed for bankruptcy, yet he is considered the father of the greatest theme parks in the world, Disney, and the creator of the most famous mouse of all, Mickey Mouse.

Oprah Winfrey overcame a tumultuous and abusive childhood. When she started her television career, she was fired from her position as a television reporter because she was considered "unfit" for TV. Nevertheless, she went on to become one of the world's most powerful and richest women in television.

Abraham Lincoln, one of my favorites, was defeated for the state legislature, failed as a businessman, had a nervous breakdown, defeated as Speaker, defeated for nomination for Congress, rejected for land officer, defeated for the US Senate twice, and defeated for nomination for vice president. Nevertheless, he went on to be elected as the sixteenth president of the United States of America.

These were all ordinary people before they became extraordinary. It was through their experiences—one failure after another—that they became great and successful. Overcoming your failures and defeats and reaching for success will require you to reach past the struggle, go deep inside to the depths of your inner strengths, and pull up all that you have left. You will have to reach past the disappointments and the dread of starting all over again, sometimes from scratch. It's okay; you can start again. When I started writing this section of my book, I had been rejected several times for a career promotion that I had been seeking for a couple of years. Nevertheless, my faith remained strong because I held on to my confidence that I possessed the required knowledge, skills, and abilities to succeed in this career. It is unfortunate that those who rejected me did not realize that they missed a great opportunity to know me and my work. More important, they missed the benefit of the positive impact I would have contributed to their organizations. Nevertheless, I learned quite well how to apply what Jack Canfield call the SW-SW-SW-SW-N principle ("*some will, some won't, so what, someone's waiting—next*") when you are rejected for an opportunity (The Success Principles).

When rejection comes, and it will come, you must realize that your greatest victory will often be the one that was the most difficult to attain. As you study story after story about the lives of great and successful people, you will find that they often faced great defeats, yet they still achieved great successes in spite of setbacks, rejections, disappointments, defeats, and failures. They succeeded only because they did not give up in the face of failure and rejection. In fact, you could say they continually failed their way to the top. When you are able to embrace your mistakes, failures, disappointments, and defeats and use them as stepping-stones, you will be on your way to reaching your greatest potential in every aspect of your life. Your road to success will be paved with many failures, setbacks, rejections, frustrations, and disappointments, but it is this same road that will also be paved with some of your greatest and most wonderful learning experiences. If you allow your challenges and negative experiences to become your stepping-stones, they will ultimately lead you to the great victories that you may never have thought possible for you. Hang in there and keep trying; your success is often closer than it seems. Every failure brings with it the opportunity to succeed.

Personal Individual Action: Using Your Failures as Stepping-Stones

Set aside some time to reflect and meditate on some of your most challenging defeats and answer these questions. What opportunities did life deny you? Are these still worthy goals for your life? What contributed most to your inability to obtain these aspirations? What do you intend to do about it?

ACTION GOAL

Answer the above questions noting what was going on in your life during these experiences. Note any life lessons you learned from these experiences. How will you use these life experiences as stepping-stones to help you achieve greatness in your life as you travel this new journey of success?

Where do these learned experiences fit within your personal self-assessment (personal, academic, career, financial, and/or giving aspirations)?

Askers, Seekers, and Knockers Do Not Allow a Difficult Beginning in Life to Dictate Their End

> Don't sit down and wait for the opportunities to come; you have to get up and make them.
>
> —Madam C. J. Walker

Life is both hard and difficult for almost everyone, and you are no exception. But despite the obstacles in your pathway, you can overcome them, no matter your station in life. Perhaps you are poor or wealthy, successful or not successful, young or old, disabled or not disabled—everyone encounters difficulties and challenges, albeit the challenges may be different. Don't let a difficult beginning dictate your middle and ending. A few years ago, I was the guest speaker for a Black History Month program. In my preparation for the speech, I focused on African American entrepreneurs who had beaten insurmountable odds and gone from poverty-stricken lives to achieving astonishing success in business and financial matters. I chose to speak about one of my historical "she-roes," Madam C. J. Walker. In her own words, she stated,

> *I am a woman who came from the cotton fields of the South. From there I was promoted to the washtub. From there I was promoted to the cook kitchen. And from there I promoted myself into the business of manufacturing hair goods and preparations.… I have built my own factory on my own ground.*

Madam C. J. Walker is a remarkable example of overcoming obstacles. She was born free as Sarah Breedlove in December 1867 on a plantation in Delta, Louisiana, approximately two years after the official ending date of slavery, December 6, 1865, the date the Thirteenth Amendment was ratified. She grew up in an era in American history when life was difficult for many people, especially those of African American descent. Nevertheless, through her dedicated persistence, perseverance, and tenacity, she overcame the life of an orphan, abuse, poverty, and widowhood to become one of the twentieth century's most successful, self-made women entrepreneurs and the first black female millionaire. She accumulated her wealth with the discovery and introduction of ground-breaking hair-care products for black women. She overcame a difficult beginning starting out as a washer woman making no more than $1.50 per week. Defying all the odds against her, she made her fortune in spite of the difficult times she was born into. Madam Walker did not take life lying down; instead, she was a fighter, and she turned her struggles into her opportunities and triumphs. I recommend that you read more about this incredible woman ("Madam Walker Essay" from www.madamcjwalker.com by A'Lelia Bundles). Much about Madam's life is told in the words of her great-great-granddaughter A'Lelia Bundles in the book titled *On Her Own Ground: The Life and Times of Madam C. J. Walker.* An excellent read, and I highly recommend it.

To overcome your own life challenges you will need to have the spirit of a Madam C. J. Walker. Without a doubt, you can possess the same level of dedicated persistence, perseverance, and tenacity as exhibited by this inspiring figure in history. It is this type of spunk that will make you get up, get busy, and reclaim the life that you have allowed to be stolen from you by seen and unforeseen forces. You have the ability to turn your greatest adversities into your greatest opportunities. Get rid of the "woe is me" attitude and start fighting for your success. Just as the life of the caterpillar who has to fight its way out of the cocoon before it can successfully turn into a beautiful butterfly, so will you have to fight for your success. Without the struggle, the caterpillar would never develop a strong body and strong wings capable of lifting it to great heights. Without the struggles that prepare the caterpillar's wings for life's challenges, it would be doomed to low-level living, unable to move from ground level. It is life's many struggles that push and prod us until we grow and develop into the beautiful, successful people we were born to be.

Everyone wants a great and easy life with as little adversity as possible. We want to be happy, have great children, a great spouse, and all the financial wealth that we can stand. Unfortunately, life is a struggle for most of us, but it is these struggles that prepare us for the trials and tribulations we must face in life. You cannot get to success without a fight, but you are equipped to win the battle. The only way you can truly become tough enough to achieve your dreams is by getting out there on the battlefield and taking on the struggles that stand between you and that dream. Through each struggle, your character is developed, your strength is renewed, and your vision becomes clearer and more pronounced.

You may have been born into or thrust into an impoverished situation, but you do not have to live with an impoverished mentality. When you come face-to-face with a difficult beginning, life can seem overwhelming. I know that it is difficult to keep going when life keeps bringing struggle after struggle, but you have to keep getting up. Where your life goes from here is up to you. It is okay to acknowledge that your life may be hard and difficult, and it may be harder and more difficult than most; nevertheless, this is something you can control by taking 100 percent of responsibility for your circumstances. A difficult and hard life cannot become your excuse for not trying. Your life will only get better when you accept the duty to make it better. The only way you can be defeated by a difficult beginning is by not getting into and not staying in the fight until you win.

Personal Individual Action: Fighting the Good Fight for Your Success

Set aside some time to reflect and meditate on some of the many battles you have faced and conquered during your life span that focused on your struggles. Choose today to stop complaining, and instead, show great gratitude that you are still here to tell your story. Give thanks that you have a new opportunity to change your circumstances.

ACTION GOAL

Reaffirm your commitment to be strong and courageous. You have no doubt endured many hardships, but you are still here. Record at least three things you will start doing today that will help you fight the good fight in finishing this new success journey.

Where does fighting the good fight for your success fit within your personal self-assessment (personal, academic, career, financial, and/or giving aspirations)?

Askers, Seekers, and Knockers Take Life On and Choose to Be Happy—Life Is Good!

> To live happy is an inward power of the soul.
>
> —Marcus Aurelius

If you do not have it, get a zest for life, because life is a good thing to have. Learn to enjoy your life today as you are on your way to your new tomorrow. Don't wait to be happy tomorrow; you can choose to be happy right now. Happiness is a choice. There is no greater teacher than life itself. How well you learn those life lessons will dictate whether you will go around and around the same mountain before learning what you should have learned the first time around the mountain. No matter your station in life, there will be good times and tough times, sunny days and stormy days. The important thing to keep in mind is that challenging times are temporary. Remember, as long as you are breathing, life is good! Your life is meant to be enjoyed. Do not go around any longer with your head hung down and singing the blues. Decide today that you can be happy, that you can have joy, and that you can have a wonderful life. Choose to take life on in full force.

I am not saying that your life will be prefect; no one's life is perfect. What I am saying is that it is important for you to start enjoying your life right where you are, right here, right now. As you are working your way through this book and making decisions about making changes in your life, one of the most important things you will ever do is decide to get excited about who you are becoming. You can choose that your life is good and getting better. Starting right now, decide that happiness is a choice. Although currently your life and your circumstances may not be where you want them to be, do not allow the circumstances of where you are to dictate your internal mental state. Stop looking at where you are today and start looking at where you are headed. Look into your mind's eye and get excited about the new person you are becoming. You may not have the job you desire, enough money, a home in a good neighborhood, or you may be incarcerated; nevertheless, you can choose to change where you are. You can find joy in looking to the future because you are making plans today to turn your circumstance around.

I will be the first to admit that life can feel daunting at times, especially when you are trying to make a course correction. I know, because I have been there. Do not get so caught up in the changes you want to make that you forget to live in the moment of today. The changes you desire will come as long as you continue to make one successive step at a time. You heard the old adage before, "How do you eat an elephant? One bite at a time." Though the change before you may seem frightening, don't let it rob you of the magic of the journey. Take time to relax, keep a good attitude, and savor your blessings no matter how small.

When you set your mind to choose to be happy, opportunities will inevitably present themselves to you for moments of happiness and celebration—take them. And, yes, moments will also appear to try and get you off-kilter, but you are able to fight away those old foreboding feelings of defeat.

STORY TIME
My Story: My Daughter Damaged Our Relatively New Car

I am reminded of the time my daughter put a dent in the back bumper of our relatively new Grand Prix. Obviously, in the early stages of my life, as I worked to make major improvements in my life and my surroundings, I did not have much money for unexpected expenses. Even though things were turning around for me and my daughter and we were beginning to have a few better possessions, the Grand Prix being one of them, my resources were very limited, and we lived on a pretty strict budget. On this particular day, I had allowed my daughter to drop me off at work, and she kept the car for school. As fate would have it, she was backing out of a parking space and she backed into a tree stump. Because it was not a full-size tree, she could not see the shorter stump; thus, she hit it. When she came to pick me up, she solemnly told me the story of what happened. I listened carefully to her sad story, and as she was telling me what happened, I silently decided that I was not going to allow myself to get upset over a dent in the bumper of a car. When she completed the story, I asked her a few questions, ensuring that she was fine, and I then simply said to her, "Okay, let us go home." Sometime later she told me that she was so frightened about damaging the car and could not imagine how I was going to react to the situation. She said that when I did not get upset, she couldn't figure out what happened. The truth is, I chose to take control of my emotions and not allow them to rule me. I decided not to lose my peace but instead to find joy in the fact that my child was safe.

You have decided to take this journey now, and even though you are not where you want to be and things are not as you desire them to be, the choice is yours to take life on one step at a time and choose to enjoy this journey. No matter how tough your days may get, you can always find a simple pleasure to appreciate in your life if you choose to. You can't make a person hire you, you can't make your boss give you a raise or a promotion, you can't control the weather, and in fact, you have no control over anyone or any external events, but you can control your emotions and your attitude. In spite of the circumstances you may be facing on the job or in your own home, whether things are good or bad, you can choose to inject joy into your life. The ability to choose to be happy can be one of your greatest assets you possess as you step out to change your circumstances.

Personal Individual Action: Happiness Is a Choice, but Joy Is an Abiding Gift

Set aside some time to reflect and meditate on some of the happiest and joyous times of your life, reflecting on what was going on that brought such an experience. No matter what you may face, you have the ability to choose not to lose your joy. Happiness may be a fleeting feeling that comes and goes, but joy is an enduring and abiding quality that is always waiting for you to return to it.

ACTION GOAL

Record how you will allow joy and happiness to become a continuous part of your reality. You have the ability to choose to create the space in your life for joy and happiness. List at least two or three things you are in control of that you can start doing today that will help you maintain your inward peace and contentment no matter what challenges you face.

Where does joy and happiness fit within your personal self-assessment (personal, academic, career, financial, and/or giving aspirations)?

Askers, Seekers, and Knockers Know that Adversity Is a Natural Part of Living

> Life challenges are not supposed to paralyze you; they are supposed to help you discover who you are.
>
> —Bernice Reagon

Adversity is a natural part of living, and oh how we wish it wasn't so! There will be times when it seems that everything just simply falls apart. Life brings with it diverse kinds of issues, often referred to as adversities. Many adversities we face are brought on by our own choices, some by other people's choices, and some simply because life happens. Nevertheless, through each adversity we can be strengthened and we are forever changed, hopefully for the better. New knowledge is gained and new experiences lived. We cry about hurts, complain about betrayals, and grieve the loss of loved ones. Yet we can look back on adversities and find laughter and joy in remembering circumstances and the people that touched and influenced us most in a positive way as we faced these challenges. A sign of maturity is how well we handle the adversities of life. The same way your physical body is developed through exercise and stretching, your character and mental state is shaped and developed through each challenging situation you encounter. In every adversity there is a new opportunity to succeed, albeit may be disguised as misfortune.

As painful as adversities may be, they are an unavoidable part of life; we all have them. When you come face-to-face with adversity, the only thing to be done is embrace the realization that you are equipped to handle it. Yes, you will be changed by events, and it is a natural progression that can strengthen you on the path of life. The more painful the adversity, the longer the healing process may take. Be patient with yourself and allow the recovery process to take as long as necessary, but don't let it overtake you. When facing adversity, you will have two choices. You can either become a martyr or choose to be an overcomer; hopefully, you will choose the latter. What would life be without adversity? You would never come to realize the inner strengths you possess and your unique ability to rise out of the ashes of adversity and become a brand-new person, stronger and more resilient than before, rising from the ashes of adversity to a new beginning.

STORY TIME
My Story: The Death of a Loving Mother

The death of my mother was the most painful adversity that I have ever faced. I was nineteen years old and had just moved to Little Rock, Arkansas, to attend business school when my mother passed. The death of my mother was a devastating blow. The depth of sadness and emptiness was incomparable, and it lingered with me for many, many years. The emotional scars suffered from losing a beloved mother at such a young age left their indelible marks on my life. However, I did not have much time to linger in my sadness because my mother left behind a husband (my father) and five other children younger than me. I faced the adversity of losing my mother by making a difficult personal decision. Since I was the oldest unmarried daughter at that time, it seemed that the most appropriate thing for me to do was to leave school, return to my hometown of Cotton Plant, Arkansas, and help my father raise my younger siblings. That is exactly what I chose to do. The operative word here is I voluntarily chose to do this. No one pressured me into making that decision.

Even though my father was grateful for my decision to return home, he questioned my decision as he wanted to be sure that I knew what I was doing. Even though the decision to return home to help my father took my personal plans off track for a while, this was one of the better decisions I made in my life. The experience brought with it a level of maturity, strength, wisdom, and an appreciation for life that I could not have gained any other way. This decision also played a significant role in helping me to come to terms with the devastating loss of my mother.

It is amazing to me the powerful inner strength we possess, even at a young age, that arises in us when we need it. Adversity can bring both joy and sadness all at the same time. Though there was sadness with the loss of my mother, there were then and still are many wonderful and happy memories I have that were birthed from returning home. When we successfully come through a trying ordeal, as difficult as it may have been, hopefully, when we look back on it and reminisce with others about the matter, we are able to point to a resilience that was birthed through the experience. If we allow ourselves, we can find a sense of pride when speaking of the new courage and strength we found and about how the experience shaped us for the better. It is these experiences, one after another, that implant in us the confidence that we will be okay, that we are powerful, that we are conquerors, and that we will survive no matter how difficult the journey. You are destined to live in victory; your adversities will only make you stronger and more courageous, if you allow them to.

Personal Individual Action: Letting Go

Set aside some time to reflect and meditate on the major adversities that you have faced in your life. Reflect on the new strengths and courage you developed as you went through those experiences. These are the values you should hold on to, but let go of the pain and other negative experiences associated with them. Part of the healing process is learning to let go of the negative experiences and cherishing the positive experiences. While both are part of who you are, it is time to let go of the negative experiences and affirm your commitment to move forward.

ACTION GOAL

Record in your journal those strengths you developed as you went through any major adversities in your life.

Where do these strengths fit within your personal self-assessment (personal, academic, career, financial, and/or giving aspirations)?

Part Six: Askers, Seekers, and Knockers Accepts No Excuses

- Askers, Seekers, and Knockers Do Not Allow Attitudinal Barriers to Rob Them of Opportunities
- Askers, Seekers, and Knockers Set High Self-Expectations
- Askers, Seekers, and Knockers Show up to Work Every day with A High Performance Attitude
- Askers, Seekers, and Knockers Are Passionate About Their Profession
- Askers, Seekers, and Knockers Do Not allow Changes in Personal Status to Become Stumbling Blocks

Askers, Seekers, and Knockers Do Not Allow Attitudinal Barriers to Rob Them of Opportunities

> There are no constraints on the human mind, no walls around the human spirit, no barriers to our progress except those we ourselves erect.
> —Ronald Reagan

What a wonderful world it would be if every day we could wake up in a universe where everyone is pleasant, full of life's vigor, and armed with a positive outlook on life, their surroundings, and the people they love. A world where there are no barriers that separate us, a world where there is no discrimination. However, the truth is we do not live in a perfect utopia where everything always comes up roses. We live in a very real world with many challenges.

Most of us face and must overcome many different types of barriers every day, some real, some visible, some invisible, some perceived, some attitudinal, some societal, and some of our own making. Nevertheless, unless barriers are correctly identified and eliminated, no matter the circumstances, they could prevent you from achieving your full potential. Barriers are those things that stand between you and what you desire to achieve. You and you alone are responsible for identifying and eliminating anything in your life that stands between you and your success, such as getting a good education, producing stable finances, and having professional and personal development.

Your success depends on you, and you cannot afford to allow yourself to develop a victim mentality. A victim mentality is blaming

145

society and other external factors for your inability to achieve what you desire. A victim type of attitude can bind you to a life of endless fighting, dissatisfaction, poverty, and unhappiness. People who play the victim game are always "going to do something when things change." They believe they are powerless to change their own circumstances, so they wait on other people to fix the world for them. They will say things like, "As soon as things get better, I am going to go back to school, going to find a job, going to leave this broken relationship, going to start going to church." They spend their entire life "going to" and "planning to fix" and never achieving. They never get around to utilizing the great unused potential that they possess and could have used to change themselves and the world around them.

If you sit around moping and allowing society to define who you are and what your station in life should be because of some meritless factor, you will live your life oblivious to what you could have achieved. You simply cannot allow barriers to get in your way and stop you from walking in your destiny.

I understand that most of us live and work in a taxing society where we may face many obstacles on a daily basis, and we all have our limitation. It is indeed true that inequalities exist in this life. However, these challenges and limitations cannot become our excuses for not working to be an overcomer and achieve great success in spite of those barriers. If you work long and hard enough, you can achieve your goals and objectives regardless of any barriers that may be erected in your path.

We have studied stories after stories about individuals who overcame insurmountable odds even in a time of great prejudices even when the very social laws on the books were against them. Yet and even still, they overcame numerous barriers to achieve great success. This is about becoming the master of your own destiny. This is about carpe diem by seizing the day through preparation by developing specific skill sets, abilities, habits, and the right attitude for achieving greatness.

Look at America today where Barack Hussein Obama was elected this nation's first African American president. Who could have seen this in 1918, the year my father was born? I am fully aware that many cultural conscious and unconscious biases continue to exist in our society. Nevertheless, it is important for you to examine yourself and consider what you may be doing or not doing that could be impeding your own progress. Yes, it may take some of us longer to reach our long-term goals. Perhaps it is because we have been forced to deal with societal and attitudinal barriers. But instead of being broken by these experiences, allow them to make you stronger. Because of your path in life, your life experiences can be richer, deeper, and more expansive. Your knowledge is perhaps broader, your problem-solving skills perhaps more vast, your coping skills sharper, and your character is above reproach. You are better because you are left with a knowing that nothing can hold you back.

I certainly was not born into a privileged family; nevertheless, my parents were God-fearing, honest, hardworking people who passed on those values to their children. While I have experienced numerous disappointments in my career, being denied employment and promotions, and suffered rejections, I have tried my best to never allow these minor setbacks to dictate my capabilities. I have not allowed a difficult beginning, my race, my gender, or any other factor to stand between me and what I believe I deserve from this life. Most successful and wealthy people in the world today are where they are because they took personal responsibility for their own success. Oprah did not allow her race, ethnicity, her gender, or society's negative attitude about her to become a barrier. She challenged the status quo and tore down the barriers that stood in her path to numerous achievements. Now, today she is the successful owner of her own television station. This is a woman who was told she would never be successful in the world of television. She did not allow the world to define her; she decided to do that herself.

In my line of work, I am amazed at how many people are not willing to assume personal responsibility for their own success by working to eliminate what they perceive as challenges that they encounter in the workplace. On the other hand, there are other individuals that I encounter in the workplace who face very real barriers every day. For example, people with disabilities who have successfully broken through the employment barrier and found lucrative careers for themselves. These individuals do not allow their limitations to impede their employment, advancement, education, or personal and professional growth. They face their challenges and excel not because of their disabilities, but in spite of their disabilities. I am reminded of such a young woman as this by the name of Ying Chen. Her story is narrated below.

STORY TIME
Ying's Story: Her Disability Cannot Stop Her. Ying has
not allowed her deafness to rob her of a good educa-
tion and a successful career in the federal government.

I met Ying Chen several years ago and found her to be an amazing, talented, bright, and capable young woman who happens to be deaf. Ying amazes me every day with her ability to successfully overcome the barriers of communication in a speaking world. Ying was born in China, where she became seriously ill when she was barely one year old. The results of her battle with this serious illness left her totally deaf. Ying has faced significant challenges in her life, yet she has excelled in spite of these challenges.

Ying grew up in a family where she was the only deaf person. Because there are so few schools that are equipped to deal with children who are deaf, these children are often sent to residential schools where they can get a proper education and are taught socialization and other life skills to survive in a speaking world. Ying's parents enrolled her in the Guangzhou, China, school for the deaf where she studied for several years. Ying's family eventually immigrated to New York City when she was fourteen years of age. Not only had Ying struggled to fit in within her own Chinese culture while growing up deaf; the move to New York City brought with it even greater challenges as she found herself plunged into a new country, a new culture, and having to learn American sign language, which was vastly different than Chinese sign language.

In order to learn English and receive a quality education, when Ying was sixteen years of age, she was again separated from her family. It was decided that she should attend the Model Secondary School for the Deaf in Washington, DC. This was a residential school located at the Gallaudet University Campus, which was approximately 240 miles from her family, who lived in New York. For most of her childhood and young adult life, Ying was separated from her parents, sister, brother, and other family members, seeing them only on a limited basis.

In spite of insurmountable odds, Ying successfully graduated from high school and enrolled in Gallaudet University, where she obtained a degree in computer information systems. Through her persistence, perseverance, and dedication, she was able to secure viable employment with the federal government, where she has received several promotions and managed to secure a journeyman level position in her career field. What I am most amazed about Ying is her work ethics. She is a self-starter that shows up every day for work on time with a high performance attitude toward work. The most remarkable thing about her is that when you encounter her, you see her abilities instead of her disability. She has never allowed communication barriers to impede her success. I have noticed that when she encounters a barrier, she goes to work to eliminate that barrier by raising the level of attention to it and working with and through others to eliminate the barrier. For example, in her spare time she frequently volunteers to conduct sign language classes for others, helping them overcome communication barriers with the deaf and hard of hearing.

Ying has not allowed society's attitudes about people with disabilities to become an obstacle for her. Ying is a world traveler and a fighter who refuses to let the challenges of her disability rob her of an education, a successful career, the rewards of home ownership, or any other benefits the world has to offer. Those of us without disabilities can learn much from Ying about living life to its fullest regardless of the challenges you may be born into or facing. Ying is a stellar example of turning challenges into stepping-stones to success.

Personal Individual Action: Removing Your Personal Barriers

Set aside some time to reflect and meditate on any perceived barrier that you believe has been holding you back from doing something you have wanted to do for a long time. There are things that we all can do to help improve our own opportunities in our personal and professional environments. Removing barriers starts with having a positive attitude about ourselves and the people we associate with. Next, identify and eliminate any self-defeating and self-limiting beliefs about yourself and behaviors that are impeding your ability to reach your daily goals and objectives.

ACTION GOAL

In a few simple statements, record in your journal those things you plan to do to eliminate any attitudinal barriers that may be holding you back. Only identify things that are actually within your control to fix.

How will removing these attitudinal barriers improve your personal self-assessment (personal, academic, career, financial, and/or giving aspirations)?

Askers, Seekers, and Knockers Set High Self-Expectations

Our limitations and success will be based, most often, on our own expectations for ourselves. What the mind dwells upon, the body acts upon.

—Denis Waitley

The Creator of the universe has endowed you and me with the ability to move, to organize, and to make good our life (Acts 17:28). What will you do with that ability? You can begin by setting high self-expectations. Develop them, internalize them, repeat them to yourself continuously, affirm them in your spirit, and hold yourself accountable for rising to the level of your personal expectations. Just as you want excellence from others, you must demand the same level of excellence from yourself, and you must be willing to pay the price to get it. Great sports teams do it, high performing organizations do it, highly successful people do it, great marriages do it, Olympians do it, and great writers do it, so why shouldn't you do it? What you can visualize and expect of yourself can become your reality. If you did not have within you the ability to achieve greatness, you would have never conceived and held that thought in your mind. Your positive personal expectations can drive you to your next level of success, if you are willing to invest the effort.

Achieving greatness requires setting the bar high, and if you intend to get from life what you believe you deserve, you will have to set your own personal high bar. This requires holding yourself personally responsible for the results. You must be willing to strive every day to be the best that you can possibly be. This should be evident not only in your personal life but also in your professional life. On your job, you should show up every day on time, early if possible, and never ever fall into a pattern of being late, even if it is for only five minutes. I worked as a civilian for the US Army for most of my federal career, and it developed in me a work culture that inspired timeliness in everything I set out to accomplish. One such lesson I learned was if you show up to work on time, you are already late. Your life and your work ethics should reflect that of a high performer. Your superiors, peers, and subordinates should know that you are a person of integrity and high moral standards and that you are dependable, loyal, and a dedicated performer. Always remember that people are watching you. They are looking to see if you are really the person you say you are. People want role models. They want people who can inspire them to reach for greatness, and they want great examples that they can emulate.

Setting your high self-expectations should not be an arbitrary process. This should be a deliberate objective process of self-empowerment where you establish the breadth and boundaries. This is where you identify what you can accomplish with vision, dedication, and hard work. Most important, this is where you give yourself permission to change your life and make it happen. Setting your own personal high self-expectations is the basic fundamental step in your personal journey for turning your challenges into triumphs. It requires clear thought, vision, planning, and preparation. Just as you would lay out a clear plan of action if you were supervising or leading a team of high performers to achieve a particular objective, you should do no less for yourself. The people you lead or supervise will rise to your level of expectation of them. More important, the children you raise and the people you influence will also rise to the level of your expectations if they see you rise. If you set the standard and expect them to achieve greatness, they will. If you expect mediocrity from them, mediocrity you will get. The same is true for yourself. What you expect of yourself will come to pass. Your self-expectations must be internalized and communicated to yourself repeatedly. This is akin to the self-fulfilling prophecy, which in essence says that your predictions about yourself will become true through the reinforcement of either positive or negative feedback between your behaviors, beliefs, and self-speak, thereby causing your expectations of yourself to be fulfilled. Everything that you will ever become is first conceived in your thoughts; therefore, knowing what you desire is the beginning.

Successful people and successful organizations set high standards, and they set out to achieve them through continuous self-improvements. For many years, as I have studied and observed successful individuals, employees, employers, and organizations, a truth that remains consistent is they set high expectations. As I have repeated over and over again in this book, successful people hold themselves accountable for success. Even when they sometimes miss the mark, they regroup, examine why they missed the mark, and reset their high expectations and embark upon the journey again and again until their objectives are accomplished. Setting high expectations for yourself is the best guarantor you have for achieving success in every area of focus in your life, yet many people fail to do so. Perhaps because it is really, really hard and requires consistent work to do this. This requires clarity of vision, planning, investment of your time and energy, and monitoring your accomplishments. This is the foundation of any successful individual, group, team, or organization.

Setting high expectations for yourself also means recognizing your own strengths and weaknesses. You must raise your standards to a level that requires you to push and stretch yourself, but at the same time, there must be balance between your expectations and what you can actually achieve. Good judgment is key in this balancing process. In the pushing and stretching process, you will find growth, and in growth, there are always personal improvements, and with personal improvements comes great personal satisfaction.

It is just as important that you build in consequences for not following your path of high self-expectations that you set for yourself. When you do that, you will strive and rise to the level of the expectation that you establish for yourself. As you go through this process, you will come to realize that what you expect of yourself is more important to you than what others think of you. Your high self-expectations must be directly linked to your goals that you established for your life. You should be able to easily identify when you are slipping off your clearly defined path to success. Be sure to implement a course correction swiftly and decisively. Success will bring celebrations and rewards, but failing to stay on your path should bring self-imposed consequences.

Just as important, remember to be flexible where necessity dictates. Sometimes your priorities may change, unforeseen circumstances may happen, and you may find it necessary to realign your goals, objectives, and expectations. There will be times when life's circumstances will dictate a change. Setting high self-expectations and living up to those expectations is not an easy overnight process; this will take time. It is a continuous process, but you can reach your destination over time by staying on the clear path that you establish for yourself. Always remember to encourage yourself frequently through personal self-affirmation. A time or two will come when you will feel discouraged and you may feel that you are on this path alone. That's okay; use these times as an opportunity to encourage yourself. Another of my favorite Bible characters is David. I find encouragement in reading about his life and accomplishments. When David found himself facing inconceivable distress and his people turned against him, although he felt alone, he encouraged himself in the Lord. Reread your personal individual actions and find strength in the renewed commitments you have made and take time to celebrate and build yourself up either with family, with friends, or in the solitude of your meditations.

STORY TIME
My Story: High School Graduation Day
and the "I Dare You" Challenge

As more and more people become familiar with my life story, I am frequently bombarded with some poignant questions. Questions such as, "What made the difference in your life? What caused you to continue your education even when times were tough? What made you fight so hard to obtain the highest levels of your professional career? Etc." There have been many factors that have influenced my choices and decisions. Many good and some not so good. But my Creator always strategically placed people along my pathway who encouraged me. Two memorable events that had a lasting impact on my young life happened when I graduated from high school. One, I was the first child in my family to graduate from high school. That day lives on as a very special and significant turning point in my life. The second significant event happened during the graduation ceremony. During the ceremony, my high school homeroom teacher, Mrs. Jamison, called me to the stage and presented me with a small burgundy book with the gold lettering *I Dare You*. During that moment, Mrs. Jamison, right there on the stage in front of everybody, dared me and challenged me to do something with my life. I was eighteen years of age at that time, and I can still remember very clearly that day and her challenge to me. Never ever underestimate the power of words and the influence of a teacher in a child's life. That challenge ignited a small flame in my spirit that still burns brightly today. It caused me to BELIEVE. That day I believed that I could achieve anything. I learned to believe that if other people could change their circumstances, why couldn't I? Mrs. Jamison had high expectations of me, and her words challenged me to set high expectations for myself. Because she believed in me, she inspired me to believe in myself. The "I dare you" challenge continues to inspire and empower me even today. My challenge to every person who reads this book is that you never underestimate the power of your influence as you touch the lives of others, especially young people. Never pass up an opportunity to encourage, inspire, and empower people by expecting greatness from them. Today, I am far from the age of eighteen, yet my life is still impacted by a great teacher that left her legacy upon my life.

Personal Individual Action: Identifying Your "I Dare You" Point(s) in History

Set aside some time to reflect and meditate on a time in your life when someone or something positively inspired you. This could have been in your early years, teenage years, and/or your adult life. These are people or events that have been strategically placed on your path of life. Their influence in your life was so impacting that it may have changed the course of your life or planted a seed in you that is still growing today. Would you classify these as your "I dare you" encounters?

ACTION GOAL

In a few simple statements, record in your journal how your life was changed or should have changed for the better because of the above encounters. What are you doing differently with your life or should be doing because of your "I dare you" encounters?

Where do your "I dare you" encounters fit within your personal self-assessment (personal, academic, career, financial, and/or giving aspirations)?

Askers, Seekers, and Knockers Show Up to Work Every Day with a High Performance Attitude

> Good enough is not always good enough.
>
> —CJM

High performance is about balance—knowing when good enough is the best possible scenario and knowing when good enough is not good enough. All of us should strive to be our very best each day whether we are serving as an employee in someone else's company, an entrepreneur working for ourselves, or working as a stay-at-home parent. Having a high performance attitude is not about being a perfectionist, but it is about not settling for mediocrity or a life of drudgery about chosen assignments. You don't have to be perfect, but you should never stop striving for perfection in your chosen profession. The work you choose should not be just to have a job so that you can make a living for yourself and your family, but rather, your work should be the thing you live to do because of the fulfillment, satisfaction, and pleasure you gain in connecting with your chosen work.

I am amazed at the number of people I have encountered who hate the jobs that they are doing. They complain about the people they work with, they complain about the organization, they complain about their work, they complain about the leadership, and they are generally miserable about coming to work every day. I wonder to myself, why do they continue to do this to themselves rather than make a change? I have even asked some this question, and they give me a myriad of excuses why they will not leave and find something different. Some of these people have been on their wrong paths for twenty to thirty years and are looking at retirement. And, I think to myself, how sad is this? Please, don't let this be your story. If you are miserable on your job every day, do something about changing your path. You cannot have an attitude of high performance if you hate your job and the people you work with.

Throughout my career, I also have encountered far too many people who are more interested in "pretending at being" rather than "actually being" the person they are pretending to be by doing the hard work. Don't be that person who never actually is as involved as they appear to be. These are the people who create the appearance of important involvement. Don't be that person who cares more about appearing as if they are the best and the brightest in their chosen profession rather than actually being the best and the brightest in their profession. Don't be that person who is only interested in keeping up appearances and looking the part of success rather than being a success. We have to walk the talk by being who we say we are on the job and off the job. True high achievers actually do the hard stuff. They are willing to do the hard labor that is usually not seen by others. They read and digest the rules of the game to the point that they become experts in their chosen professions. Because of their expertise, others frequently seek them out for guidance and directions and the big promotions.

For those who truly want to achieve all that life has to offer, they realize that they have to "BE" rather than "appearing to BE." They know that they have to show up for life. They show up on their jobs every day on time and with a great attitude about work. They show up as great employees, they show up as great coworkers, they show up as great leaders, they show up as great followers, and they show up as great influencers in their milieu. They show up as great spouses and great parents. They show up as reliable friends and relatives—they show up! They realize that there are no shortcuts to real success.

There will be times when you will outgrow your current assignments. When this occurs, don't be afraid to bid for the next opportunity that will allow you to continue to grow both professionally and personally. This may mean changing careers, changing agencies, changing organizations, or relocating to a new city or state. Sometimes when you stay too long in the same assignment when you have outgrown it, complacency tends to set in, and then it becomes easier to embrace an attitude of "this is good enough." Settling for good enough could result in no new experiences being gained, development becomes stagnated, and opportunities for advancement ceases. Even though the individual knows that it is probably a good idea to move on, they usually will not because this has become their comfort zone for a myriad of reasons. If this is you, you could miss a great opportunity to rise to the next level of success.

High performers who feel great about their workplaces will accumulate both annual and sick leave balances to be used when necessity dictates. They do not use up every hour of sick and annual leave as soon as it accrues, and when emergency situations come around they, find themselves in a hard situation. Individuals with a high performance attitude and great work ethics stand out far above individuals who simply show up for a paycheck. High performers recognize their strengths and weaknesses. It is this type of work ethic and high performance attitude that separates "appearing to be" from "actually being."

They recognize that good enough is not always good enough if they are going to rise to their fullest potential. They address their beliefs, assumptions, and any self-defeating behaviors that impede their ability to advance to the next level. They recognize that what was acceptable performance a year ago may now need to rise to a new level in order to continually move in a direction of continuous self-development. However, it is just as important to recognize when your performance and progress has achieved its optimum level and it's time to move on, or the individual gets marred down in minuscule details that add no real value to the individual's professional or personal growth.

When you embrace the concept of being a high performer with an excellent work ethic, you may have to walk a lonely road by doing things that few of your peers are willing to do. You will have to stretch yourself to reach for the next level. You may have to take on the tough challenges no one else wants—staying late, arriving early, disciplining yourself, traveling more often, and not partying with the group at the end of the day. You may be accused of setting standards that are too difficult to achieve, but you will continue to push forward anyway because you know that a great reward is at the end of a difficult and challenging road.

Personal Individual Action: Identifying Your High Performance Attitude

Set aside some time to reflect and meditate on the areas of your life where you clearly exhibit an attitude of high performance. Is this high performance exhibited on your job, in your home, in extracurricular activities, in charity work, in your religious profession? Is it possible that the reason why you experience an attitude of high performance in this particular area is that this is what connects you to your purpose? Is this an aha moment for you?

ACTION GOAL

In a few simple statements, record in your journal how and where your attitude of high performance shows up the strongest. Do you need to make any course corrections in this area?

Where does your attitude of high performance fit within your personal self-assessment (personal, academic, career, financial, and/ or giving aspirations)?

Askers, Seekers, and Knockers Are Passionate About Their Chosen Profession

> Choose a job you love, and you will never have to work a day in your life.
>
> —Confucius

The above quote is profound on its very face. This is how I feel about my profession, and this is how you will feel about your profession when it connects you with your purpose. In the work that I do every day, I honestly cannot tell you where I end and my profession begins. I am so intertwined with my career that my work and my spirit flows in harmony. This is the energy that excites me about getting out of bed, fighting traffic, and showing up at work every day and looking forward to performing to the best of my ability. I cannot overemphasize how important it is for you to choose the type of work that connects you to your purpose so that you too can enjoy the work you do every day. When you enjoy your work, it is no longer work, and when you find pleasure in your work, it is not difficult to perfect it.

To have a positive relationship with your chosen profession, whether it is in the home or outside of the home, is an excellent motivator for gearing you up to face the challenges of a workweek. Askers, Seekers, and Knockers value their careers. To rise five days out of seven, get dressed, fight traffic, and show up on time day after day, excited about doing what you get to do, should be your goal. To love what you do, to use your talents, strengths, and abilities in order that you may make a difference in the world and the life of others is a worthy goal indeed.

Being passionate about your chosen profession encompasses far more than a job title, a particular career path, or a salary. Career passion is about whether you love and enjoy what you do, bringing with it a sense of consistent satisfaction. It does not matter whether you are a homemaker, a member of the military, a secretary, a custodial worker, the CEO of a powerful company, the owner of your own business, or the president of the United States. What matters is whether you are fully satisfied with where you are. If you are given the opportunity to use your inborn talents and skills to accomplish your daily duties and responsibilities, it should show in your performance. People that you encounter will see your passion represented in the accomplishments of your goals and objectives. Do not get me wrong; I understand that no one will love his or her job every day. There will be days when you will feel like the song that says, "Take this job and shove it," but for the most part, hopefully those days will be few and far between. Your workdays are a lot easier when you figure out what you are good at and go after it with your full passion.

When I speak of being passionate about your profession, I am speaking about having a sense of harmonious satisfaction with what you do on a daily basis. I have worked in both private and federal sector careers, and what I have found to be consistently true is that the majority of people who are fulfilled and engaged in their work are those who are competent in their line of work. They all have several common characteristics. They feel their assignments are challenging, they have a great deal of autonomy in their positions, and they have a positive influence in their workplace. They believe that they are valued, respected, and have the opportunity to use what they have for the good of the workplace. If this does not sound like you and you are no longer feeling passionate about your career choices, perhaps it is time to make different choices.

Take a look at your career and ask yourself this very basic question, "Am I happy and fulfilled doing what I do every day in my career?" If your response is no to that basic question, you have some decisions to make; it is as simple as that. If your heart is not in what you are doing, the passion will not be there either. Are you measuring success in your life by a job or career title, by the amount of money you make, or by the fulfillment of being able to utilize the abilities that make you who you are? Only you can truthfully answer that question. Listen to what your heart is saying to you. Your energy is released, you are more productive, and you perform better when you are doing the things that you are passionate about. At the end of your career and facing retirement, will you be one of those people who will end up someday saying "I should have" or "If only I had." My friend the late Millie Steel had a favorite phrase for people who lamented over waiting too late to take the necessary actions for their life. She would say to them, *"Don't should on yourself—just do what you know you need to do."* I absolutely agree with Millie because life is too short to suffer in a job or a career where you find little satisfaction. Furthermore, your family and the world may never come to know that special gift that you have hidden inside of you that could have made a difference in the lives of so many people if you fail to use it.

Many, many people have changed unfulfilling careers and professions, no matter how great the pay, because they were unfilled in what they were doing. You have to love what you do, love the people you work with, or make the necessary changes that will help you recharge and find fulfillment. Let us say you are not very happy with your current job and you are not in a position to walk away from the job you are on; then seek ways to create opportunities for yourself that will help bring satisfaction to your profession. Remember the old axiom, "When you get lemons, make lemonade." Try some of these suggestions as these are things that worked for me. Seek opportunities for more autonomy where you can make more independent decisions about how the job is to be accomplished. Shape your work environment by becoming more engaged in the organization and by integrating elements of what you are passionate about into your everyday routine. Volunteer to take on more challenging assignments; this could open up more doors for advancement. Volunteer to take on collateral duty assignments that will allow you to use your talents more effectively. Interact more with peers and the leadership team through making meaningful contributions. If the people you work with every day are not much fun to be around, look for working groups or committees that you can join who are made up of energetic people that you are more closely aligned with. Seek opportunities for new and challenging assignments that will allow you to utilize your skills and abilities in more productive ways. Work to foster a better working environment by being a living example of the core values you want to see more of, such as trustworthiness, great communication skills, flexibility, reliability, and caring. You should be the change you want to see in the world, says Mahatma Gandhi.

STORY TIME
My Story: Finding Self-Motivation Working
at Van Heusen Shirt Factory

I can honestly say that I have enjoyed most every job I ever held, that is after leaving the farm. Although I was a farm girl, I never really adored chopping and picking cotton and the rest of the labor-intensive work that goes along with living on a farm. My first real job working outside of the farm was with the Van Heusen Shirt Company, where I was assigned the job of a trimmer. From there I have worked as a secretary, a receptionist, and other administrative positions to the professional career that I have with the federal government. In these careers, I have been fortunate enough to be able to utilize my inner talents and abilities to find my niche even when the job itself was not what I really wanted to do. This has allowed me to exercise autonomy, create challenges, and get the results I aim for. That little secret has allowed me to turn any job I have held into an enjoyable work experience. When a work assignment became routine and mundane, rather than settling into complacency, I sought out different options to make it more fulfilling and enjoyable. This can be done with any position or assignment no matter how simple or complex; it only takes thought and enough resourcefulness to try.

In particularly, I am reminded of when I worked as a trimmer with Van Heusen. The job of a trimmer was a rudimentary function performed on an assembly line in a shirt factory. It offered very little opportunity for variations in how the job was to be performed; therefore, I looked to my teammate for the challenge. I still remember the challenge. The teammate was one of my childhood friends, Ms. Brenda Thomas. Actually, Brenda was a much better and faster trimmer than I was, and she had been performing the function longer than I had. My secret goal was to try and beat her production on a daily basis in order to outperform her on a weekly basis. Needless to say, there were very few occasions where I actually outperformed Brenda, but I gave her a good run for the money. Secretly paring myself against Brenda and trying to outperform her resulted in several excellent benefits. I was eager to get to work every day to see what I could do. I mastered the art of trimming, I developed an attitude of high performance, and it was overall very good for my company because I routinely exceeded my own quota. While there was no formal agreement or arrangement between me and Brenda as to my trying to outperform her, I always suspected that she knew what I was trying to do, and she was not about to let me win on a routine basis. Challenging myself this way was a great motivator, and it gave me a sense of great satisfaction. I voluntarily decided to attempt to outperform Brenda, and the competition made me a stronger performer, and it kept me from falling into a trap of complacency.

The basic lessons I learned as a factory worker, I continue to utilize in every duty assignment I have held since that time. This is the art of self-motivation and the ability to find inspiration in almost any job no matter the task. I encourage you to use your inner qualities, skills, and abilities to seek opportunities for autonomy, create challenges, and work to improve your competences in any chosen profession. Satisfaction comes from being able to use what is inside of you to accomplish the goals and objectives you create for yourself.

Personal Individual Action: Inspiration through Self-Motivation

Set aside some time to reflect and meditate on your chosen profession. Do you find satisfaction in the work you do? Do you feel that your work connects you to who you are and to your purpose? Are there other things you can do in your profession to help you find even greater fulfillment?

ACTION GOAL

In a few simple statements, record in your journal at least one thing you can do in your place of employment that can help improve the work environment for you and the people you work with.

Where does job satisfaction in your chosen profession fit within your personal self-assessment (personal, academic, career, financial, and/or giving aspirations)?

Askers, Seekers, and Knockers Do Not Allow Changes in Personal Status to Become Stumbling Blocks

> The greater the contrast, the greater the potential. Great energy only comes from a correspondingly great tension between opposites.
>
> —C. G. Jung

There will be many times when we all will face life's hard, difficult, and sometimes just downright unbearable circumstances. Some people may face unemployment, illness, underemployment, homelessness, divorce, incarceration, the loss of a loved one, or even just getting older, which all can be devastating, life-altering events. But these experiences should not destroy you; you can overcome them. You must not allow these experiences to become permanent obstacles that will pull you under the currents of life. As long as you are breathing and have life in your body, you have the ability to make these experiences become your past experiences and use them as stepping-stones to help you grow stronger and better.

As you face the difficulties of life, you will make choices that will either move you forward or hold you back. You can decide to embrace the change and transition to the next positive level or get stuck in an eternal loop of misery and a "woe is me" attitude. I am speaking from experience when I say that it is very difficult to see clearly when you are in the middle of a storm, but there are better and brighter days ahead of you. If you are going through a divorce, know this: there is life after divorce—even after two or three divorces.

One day your divorce will be a thing of the past, and you will look back and say, "I can hardly believe I was once married to that …" You can fill in the blank. (LOL.) Listen, I am not making light of tough times in your life—what I am trying to do is convenience you that if you work hard every day to change these difficult circumstances, you can rebuild your life after life-altering events.

One of the best ways to overcome your challenges is by adding value to someone else's life. It does not matter what difficult circumstance you may be facing; you still have value, and you have the ability to add value to others. If you find yourself in a homeless shelter or incarcerated, you still have value. Right where you are, you are continually interacting with other people who need to hear a word of encouragement. Sometimes it is not so much about helping yourself overcome, but rather it is about helping others to overcome that you may find your way out of a difficult situation. Often, it is during the process of valuing others that you will find your own inner strength to face your challenges. As you struggle through every challenge of life, opportunities to help others who may be less fortunate than you will always present themselves. You have the ability to offer encouragement, inspiration, enthusiasm, and value to someone who may or may not be less fortunate than you. The question is, will you reach out and help others, or will you continue to waddle in your own circumstance? It is my sincere belief that you will know which choice to make.

I want to add another note of caution: as you work your way through life's difficult challenges, watch your language. Steer away from negative, unproductive self-speak. At all cost, avoid putting yourself down and speaking negatively about yourself and your circumstances. It doesn't matter if you are where you are because of your poor choices or because of someone else's poor choices. Speak positively about your life and your future. As you face each day, look for reasons to be grateful and give thanks. Rather than complaining about the things that are still not going so well, look instead for ways to celebrate the gift of life in you. As long as you have life, you have a chance to change your circumstances. You may not realize it, but no matter where you find yourself in life, there is always someone some-where who is watching you. You may just be the inspiration someone else needs to motivate them to action in their own life.

Personal Individual Action: Stop Stumbling and Step Up

Set aside some time to reflect and meditate on areas of your life where you may be spending too much time dwelling on unfortunate incidents (stumbling blocks) that have adversely impacted your life. Think about your self-speak regarding these situations. Do you know anyone who may have experienced the same or a similar situation as your experience? Is there something you can do to help them over-come that situation?

ACTION GOAL

In a few simple statements, record in your journal what you can do and will do to turn your stumbling blocks into stepping-stones. Record what you will stop saying about yourself (negative speech) and what you will start saying about yourself (positive, encourag-ing, and uplifting speech) regarding these situations. List at least one person you will encourage and uplift who may be going through a difficult period.

Where does your letting go of your stumbling blocks and reach-ing out to encourage others fit within your personal self-assessment (personal, academic, career, financial, and/or giving aspirations)?

Part Seven: Askers, Seekers, and Knockers Care

- Askers, Seekers, and Knockers Know That Their Word Is a Binding Invisible Contract
- Askers, Seekers, and Knockers Give and Share Credit and They Assume the Responsibility when Things go Wrong
- Askers, Seekers, and Knockers Know That Honesty and Integrity Are Essential Qualities That Must Never Be Compromised
- Askers, Seekers, and Knockers Are Driven by More Than Financial Gain
- Askers, Seekers, and Knockers Know that They Must Be Unwavering in Their Convictions

Askers, Seekers, and Knockers Know that Their Word Is a Binding Invisible Contract

> Let your yes be yes and your no be no, so that you may not fall under judgment.
>
> —James 5:12

Make your word and commitments count! There are many things in this world that we cannot control, but we can control our word and our commitments. Your word is one of the most defining values that shape your character, and there is nothing that destroys a person's credibility faster than not honoring their word. Your code of ethics must be *"Do what you say you will do."* This should be our greatest pursuit. Whether you realize it or not, people are watching what you say and what you do. They are watching to see if you will honor your word and whether or not you are walking your talk. They look at your professional and personal life, your workplace, your community, your place of worship, your family, and they observe you in your social settings. We all want our actions and behavior to exemplify the character of an Asker, Seeker, and Knocker. Your word and the things you do and say are binding commitments and represent an invisible contract between you and those in your circle of influence. In fact, your words are so powerful that they also represent a binding contract between you and yourself. When we fail to honor our word, it not only impacts others, but it will begin to chip away, little by little, at what we believe about ourselves. Inner conflicts set in when we do not believe the words that are coming out of our own mouth. It is equally important that our words have integrity in small things just as in big things. People are listening to our words, but they will watch our deeds to determine whether our words and actions are congruent.

Unfortunately, we live in a society where there are far too many Bernie Madoffs and other people whose words are of no account. Because of this, they have caused great harm to themselves and to people who trusted them. People have suffered bankruptcies, lost pension funds, lost retirements accounts, made bad investments, suffered divorces, lost families and homes, all because they trusted in something or in someone that proved unworthy of that trust and confidence. Each time someone gives their word and fail to honor it, a bit of their integrity is chipped away. Each time someone compromises their integrity and fail to do what they say they will do, a bit of trust is lost until finally those individuals are viewed as untrustworthy.

Obviously, there will come a time when you too will not be able to keep your word on a matter, or you may find that you can no longer honor a commitment that you have made. When this happens, face that individual, explain the circumstance, and clarify why you will not be able to honor your word on that particular matter. Try to make a different arrangement where you will be able to follow through and honor your word regarding that particular matter at a later time. You should make the first move and resolve this before the person has to confront you. Yes, no doubt a little bit of trust in you will be lost, but you can earn it back. It is imperative that you step forward and let the person know up front that you have to change what you initially promised.

On your journey to achieving success, you will need other people to make things happen in your life, and likewise, people will need and depend on you to make things happen for them. Without each other, we are nothing. You need others for support just as they need you for support. It is the reliance and dependence upon one another and our word to each other that will catapult each of us to our own successes. If you want people to trust you and your word to count for something, develop a habit of overdelivering on your promises. People will appreciate and never forget what you did. You will have created value above what was expected, and they will always cherish your generosity. No matter how tired you get or that you have a limited schedule, if you give your word to do something, make it happen every time—not sometimes and not most of the time, but every time. This will inspire confidence in the people that you influence, and they will see from your actions that you are a person of integrity. They will know that you are a person worthy of their trust, one who can be counted on time after time to honor your commitments. Your influence in the lives of others is broader than you may think.

Personal Individual Action: Influencing Others through Honoring Commitments

Set aside some time to reflect and meditate on areas of your life where you can enhance your reputation with others by improving on how you honor and keep your commitments. Think about these things: Do I treat others in the same manner that I want them to treat me? Do I place other people's concerns ahead of mine, or am I the preferred choice? When I give my word, do I honor it 100 percent of the time, 75 percent of the time, 50 percent of the time, 25 percent of the time, or is it sometimes I do and sometimes I don't?

ACTION GOAL

In a few simple statements, record in your journal what you can and will do to improve in those areas that require attention. To be thought of as a person of great character with a stellar reputation and one who honors commitments is better than wearing a crown of jewels. A crown of jewels can be stolen away by a robber, but a good reputation and an honorable character can never be stolen from you; it can only be given away by you.

Where does honoring your word and your commitments fit within your personal self-assessment (personal, academic, career, financial, and/or giving aspirations)?

Askers, Seekers, and Knockers Give and Share Credit and They Assume Responsibility When Things Go Wrong

> The more credit you give away, the more will come back to you. The more you help others, the more they will want to help you.
>
> —Brian Tracy

"People first; mission always." Retired General Robert Flowers (Corps of Engineers) taught me those important words. Through his leadership, he demonstrated that taking care of people is the most important aspect of what we do every day. In their personal and professional lives, Askers, Seekers, and Knockers give and share credit when things are going well, and they shoulder the responsibility when things go wrong. We are all interconnected, and no matter what we do in life, it is impossible to accomplish our goals and objectives without reliance on each other. Caring is a quintessential aspect of relationship building. One of the best ways to demonstrate caring is through valuing people for who they are and for what they bring to the relationship, whether it is in a professional, personal, or spiritual nature. Everyone values appreciation and recognition, and everyone, without exception, appreciates being recognized for who they are and for their contributions. People desire to feel valued and respected; don't ever pass up an opportunity to make others feel important and esteemed. Constantly look for what others are doing right and build them up by inspiring them to achieve greatness. Try to do this with children, spouses, parents, coworkers, partners, and especially with those you lead. Caring, valuing, and respecting people will generally inspire them to strive even more to achieve their own greatness.

One sure way of showing others that you respect and value them is by giving and sharing credit where credit is due and maybe even sometimes when it may not be due. Giving credit for ideas, accomplishments, and contributions is an excellent motivator. This is especially important to do in the home and work environments. Giving credit goes a long way; even giving credit for small things is a way of inspiring an individual to strive to do more and greater things. Taking an inventory of the entire span of your career, you could probably recall a time when someone failed to give you the proper credit you deserved for your efforts and contributions to a particular project. Even if the person did not realize it at the time, it still left you feeling hurt, rejected, devalued, and underappreciated. You can never successfully accomplish your goals and objectives independent of others, whether it is in the workplace, your community, your home, or your place of worship. Our ideas and efforts are interconnected with others that we interact with on a daily basis. Your efforts will impact the success of others, and their efforts will impact your success. Therefore, it is important to equally share the credit for accomplishments.

It is important to you, to those whom you lead, and to those within your sphere of influence that you never fail to recognize and give and share credit with those who are deserving of such honor. No matter how small or how great their contributions, people want to be recognized for their efforts. While this may sound like a simple common courtesy that anyone with manners would observe, you would be amazed how frequently this courtesy is overlooked in formal and informal settings. Too frequently, the right people with remarkable contributions are overlooked, and instead others who may not be as deserving receive the credit. When people feel as though they have been slighted or not recognized for their accomplishments, they can easily feel exploited or taken advantage of, leading to feelings of mistrust. Giving and sharing credit with others for their contributions sends a message that you can be trusted. This trust is critical to building and sustaining fundamental relations that can be relied upon for current and future endeavors.

Now wait, before you become eager to start pointing fingers, stop and take a look at yourself and examine whether you have ever allowed your own personal biases to cloud your judgment and you missed an opportunity to share credit. It is your responsibility to be observant and to be on the lookout for opportunities to give recognition. Ensure that those whom you work with are recognized for the value they bring. If you are the leader in the workplace, it is especially important that you foster this type of work culture. The team you lead will look to you to set the example. Everyone should be encouraged to give and share credit among the team. On the other hand, I have seen times when people fail to speak up for themselves and take credit for the contributions they have made. Those individuals should be encouraged to own their successes and not be afraid to take and receive credit for the hard work and contributions they have made. Everyone sharing and giving credit enhances the dynamics of the entire group. By finding positive ways to demonstrate that we care about others, we add value to their lives, and we strengthen relationships. In this type of environment, performance increases, collaboration and productive relationships are forged, and creativity is experienced at a greater level. Trust and respect within groups, within marriages, within communities, and within other relationships are enhanced.

The other side of the coin to giving and sharing credit is assuming responsibility when things go wrong. Never ever throw another person under the bus or use them as a scapegoat to save your own skin. Step up and take responsibility for failures and problems. Failures and unforeseen problems are an inevitable part of people working together. When things go wrong, look to the complexities of the situation or project that may have contributed either directly or indirectly to the failure. This will prove to be a more constructive process for getting everyone involved in helping to identify what went wrong and how to fix it, rather than blaming each other. Help everyone identify something that they perhaps could have done that could have prevented the failure, and you should be the first to lead off with something you could have done better. When people see that you are willing to step up and assume responsibility and share in the failures, they will generally follow suit. You will find that taking such actions will go a long way in promoting trust and respect from those whom you lead and interact with, and better long-term relationships have a greater opportunity to be forged. In the long run, a greater level of trust will be realized between you and the people you lead and interact with.

Personal Individual Action: Caring, Sharing, and Bringing Value to Others

Set aside some time to reflect and meditate on areas of your life where you can demonstrate the art of caring, valuing others, and sharing and giving credit. Reflect on what you can do when a situation goes wrong even when it is not your fault.

ACTION GOAL

In a few simple statements, record in your journal what you can do and will do to demonstrate an attitude of caring that will help others feel valued, respected, and appreciated when things are going well and when things are not going so well.

Where does your caring, sharing, valuing, and appreciating others fit within your personal self-assessment (personal, academic, career, financial, and/or giving aspirations)?

Askers, Seekers, and Knockers Know that Honesty and Integrity Are Essential Qualities that Must Never Be Compromised

> Integrity is built by defeating the temptation to be dishonest; humility grows when we refuse to be prideful; and endurance develops every time you reject the temptation to give up.
>
> **—Rick Warren**

In today's society, it may seem that good old-fashioned honesty and integrity are values that are sometimes hard to find in many leaders, peers, families, and friends. Nevertheless, Askers, Seekers, and Knockers know that to have integrity is to be honest, and to be honest is to have integrity. These values are synonymous with each other, as you cannot truly have one without the other. We must take great pride in these values and keep them close to our hearts no matter what. Even when your surrounding circumstances change, when people fall out of your life for whatever reasons, or when tragedy hits, these values must never be sacrificed. If you are to become who you are destined to become, these values must resonate with you in every action every day! How you live significantly influences those whom you interact with, and they are watching you. Though all of us desire the finer things in life that wealth offers, if our path to riches and wealth causes us to disregard or sacrifice these important values in order to gain wealth and riches, you should immediately change the path.

Unfortunately, some people believe that the more wealth and riches they have, it will automatically bring them more joy and happiness, but this is woefully untrue. The truth is real achievements, success, and riches are found in who you will become on this journey called life. As you already know by now, it is the struggles through the storms of life and the ups and downs that test our will, build our character, enhance our values; and at the end of the day, it is those intangible qualities that bring the real victory. Our joy is found in the person we become on the journey; this is the rich life that no economic downturn can take away.

Living a life of honesty and integrity starts with you; it lies at the very core of who we all should strive to be. Attaining success is having the ability to achieve and sustain that which we desire most without losing who we are in the process. At the end of the day, real wealth and riches lie in the character of the individual. The good news is anyone can live a life of honesty and integrity. Take a personal reflection of your inner values; in your reflection, answer the question, "Do honesty and integrity play a major role in my life every day?" These values are something we all look for in those whom we interact with. We seek these values in a mate and in friends, employers seek them in applicants and applicants seek them in employers, we seek them in the medical and legal professions, and we certainly seek them in our spiritual leaders and associates.

Holding on to the values of honesty and integrity will not always be easy; sometimes it will be challenging. When temptations come, and they will come, you will have to get focused and keep your eyes on the prize of who you are striving to become. None of us have cornered the market on these values as each one of us must consistently work hard every day at being people who live by these values. My hope for every person that reads this book is that you are and shall remain people of character who display the values of honesty and integrity daily.

Personal Individual Action: Valuing Integrity and Honesty

Set aside some time to reflect and meditate on areas of your life where you can enhance the values of integrity and honesty. It could be something as simple as increasing your service to your community or doing things around your home before being asked to do them. As we display our integrity and honesty, it is important to take care of the little things in life, for it is the little foxes that spoil the vines (Song of Solomon 2:15).

ACTION GOAL

In a few simple statements, record in your journal what you can do and will do to demonstrate the values of integrity and honesty in your everyday life.

Where do the values of integrity and honesty fit within your personal self-assessment (personal, academic, career, financial, and/ or giving aspirations)?

Askers, Seekers, and Knockers Are Driven by More Than Financial Gain

> Whoever loves money never has money enough; whosoever loves wealth never has profit enough.
>
> —Ecclesiastes 5:10

When more than just the all-mighty dollar drives your motivation, it is easier to accept that success will not come overnight. Askers, Seekers, and Knockers are people who are willing to delay immediate gratification and hold out for a type of currency that cannot be blown away on a shopping spree or lost in the stock market. They resign themselves to the fact that compensation will not always follow an immediate effort. When you are working to achieve your life goals, you should settle in for a period of sacrifice and intense effort when working to perfect your craft. Real success is measured by more than mere financial gain, but rather it is about preparing to be a part of something that not only benefits you but others in the process as well.

When I worked for the Department of the Army, one of the core values taught by the Army was "selfless service." Your success must be motivated by that which is greater than personal financial gain alone. Obviously, financial gain is a great benefit, but it should not be your sole motivator. Don't get me wrong. I am not saying that financial gain is not important; I am saying that it must remain in its proper place on your journey. You should not become so focused on gaining wealth that you put aside sharing valuable time with others you enjoy being with. I know the old adage is true: money is not everything, but it does help. However, peace of mind, integrity, honesty, your values, and other intangible pleasures of life far out-weigh a constant focus on material wealth. On your success journey, you should never become so focused on gaining wealth that you lose focus of the simple pleasures in life such as relationship building, family, friends, and your physical, emotional, and mental health. It is important to take the time to do the things that you enjoy most. Striking the right balance between what you value and wealth is what you are looking for.

Take time to enjoy your journey to success. When you finally achieve the success you are seeking, you also want to be able to say that on this journey, you never sacrificed for financial gain your integrity or your relationships with those who matter most to you. You want to be able to say that you unselfishly invested in the lives of others and brought them along with you on this journey. When your journey to success has been fulfilled, you will want to have your character intact and those most important to you to be there with you to share in your success.

Earlier in the book, we discussed what success means to you; revisit your response and update it where appropriate. Always include the date of your update. This will reflect your personal growth in new knowledge gained on this journey. Whatever you have defined your success to be, it must be that thing that fulfills you. Real wealth is found in that which you possess that no one can take away from you, such as your formal knowledge gained through education and your informal knowledge gained through life experiences. Though my mother had little more than a third-grade education, she possessed an abundance of innate wisdom which she taught and demonstrated to her children. She emphasized that it is important to care about others and to value them more than material wealth. She found suc-cess in being accessible to her family and the community she lived in. She demonstrated this sense of caring through numerous random acts of kindness. This is where she was most successful and where she found her purpose in life, and this is what brought her great joy. She demonstrated that the world should be a better place simply because we lived. This is the legacy she left with me: it is important to unselfishly invest in others, not for what they can do for you, but rather, simply, for what you can do for them.

In this technologically advanced and fast-paced world that surrounds us, it is easy to lose focus of true wealth, but I can think of no greater contribution to your own success than that of being a part of and connected to the people whom you care about and who care about you. It is for these reasons that Askers, Seekers, and Knockers are driven by more than financial gain. Your gratification is the resulting effect of knowing that as you work to fulfill your own destiny, you are playing your part in the betterment of the lives of others and humanity at large. Yes, there will be periods of rewards and financial gain along the way, but real gratification will come through the legacy you leave behind that impact the lives of others and the generations that come after you.

When you are doing that which you love to do, material resources are sure to follow after great effort. As you give, you will receive back and more abundantly than which you gave out. On your success journey, don't waste your valuable time focusing only on material wealth; as you grow in your success, the benefits of success will follow you as you persistently attune your heart, mind, and spirit toward your goals and objectives.

Personal Individual Action: Putting Financial Gain in Its Proper Place

Set aside some time to reflect and meditate on areas of your life where you can become more persistent in your endeavors to accomplish the desires of your heart that reach beyond financial gain. As you consistently set your heart and mind toward your endeavors, the universe will cause opportunities and resources to gravitate toward you.

ACTION GOAL

In a few simple statements, record in your journal the amount of financial gain you desire that you believe will generate a life of comfort. Record when you plan to achieve that level of financial gain. Record what you will do to gain that level of financial gain. Rewrite this on a separate piece of paper and stick it up someplace where you can see it every day. Now, you have settled the question of what you want your financial gain to be. Now you can stop thinking about money and focus your energy more appropriately upon your actions every day that will help you become the person you desire to be who is capable of achieving and living at that level of success.

Where does settling the question of what you want your financial life to be fit within your personal self-assessment (personal, academic, career, financial, and/or giving aspirations)?

Askers, Seekers, and Knockers Know that They Must Be Unwavering in Their Convictions

> Stand for something, or you'll fall for anything.
>
> —Alexander Hamilton

First question, are you standing on your own convictions, or are you living out other people's convictions and fighting their causes because theirs seem to be more exciting than your own? Second question, are you living the life you desire to live, or are you just breathing and taking up time and space as you glide through life, letting life dictate your path rather than you charting your own course? Final question, are you living your life or someone else's life? One thing is for sure, if you do not master your life, life will master you. Living a successful and adventurous life requires you to take a stand for some things and against some things, or you will never master your life or your destiny. You cannot be masterful of your life by being against everything, and you cannot be masterful of your life by being for everything; there is a balance. Those who stand for nothing will surely fall for everything and anything; whatever ideas that come along, they will find themselves trailing behind them, oftentimes to their own detriment.

If you do not know what it is that ignites your life and brings meaning to your very existence, you have not yet begun to master your own life. If you find yourself feeling empty, annoyed, and dissatisfied with life, maybe it is time for you to listen to what your life is trying to tell you. Stop telling your life what you are going to do with it, but instead, try listening to what your life wants to do with you. Listen to that deep, still voice that often gets drowned out with the noises of life. There seems to be a bit of controversy surrounding who actually coined the phrase "*Stand for something, or you will fall for anything.*" Whether it was Peter Marshall, Alexander Hamilton, or Alex Hamilton, regardless of who first coined the phrase, no truer words have ever been spoken. There will be times when your instincts (your inner spirit) will know where you stand, long before your intellect will know. It is times like these when you will need to trust and obey your instincts when they clearly line up with your value systems, regardless of what anyone else may have to say about the situation. Do not let others sway you from a cause or from taking a stand that you truly feel and believe is part of your destiny, especially when it aligns with your life's journey.

Your legacy is and shall continue to be founded upon your level of conviction in who you are and what it is that you stand for. When you strongly believe in a worthy cause and are willing to put energy, resources, and passion into that endeavor, you will have the power to positively influence this generation and the generations to come after you. You and I both know people who exemplified strong convictions and beliefs. No matter what problems or troubles the world brought to them, they were so passionate and so unwavering in their convictions and for what they stood for that nothing could deter them and pull them off their path. Their desires burned within them, and their passion and burning desires ignited others to action and caused them to pick up their causes. Nothing could stop them, not jail, beatings, repeated failures, illness, poverty, lack, and not even death could silence their works—people like Dr. Martin Luther King, Jr., Harriet Tubman, Albert Einstein, Abraham Lincoln, Mother Teresa, and Helen Keller, to name a few.

Askers, Seekers, and Knockers must answer this question for themselves, "What do I stand for?" Listen, listen, listen. Stop and begin to listen to the still, quite voice deep within; that voice is trying to whisper to you your convictions, the desires of your heart, what you value, what you represent, and what you stand for. It is time for you to stop wondering through life and listening to every great idea or suggestion that comes along and send you on a roller-coaster ride—up one day and down the next. As great as these ideas and suggestions may seem, they amount to nothing unless they are part of your convictions and fit within your life's master plan.

In this instant microwave world with social media, "twenty-four hours, seven days a week" news cycles, and an instant awareness of everyone and everything that's happening almost instantly as it happens, life can get distracting and create a sense of sameness. This sense of sameness can easily influence you to take on another's values, ideas, vocations, convictions, and causes. All of which may very well be laudable causes, but they may not necessarily be your cause. Are you walking in your moccasins or someone else's? Stay on the path of your true north!

Personal Individual Action: Embracing Your Convictions

Set aside some time to reflect and meditate on areas of your life where you demonstrate your strong convictions. How strongly do you feel about your convictions? Do your convictions require modification? Are your convictions worth living for, and are they worth dying for? Every person should be willing to make a sacrifice for what they really and truly believe in.

ACTION GOAL

In a few simple statements, record in your journal something that you can do and will do to enhance your level of commitment to your convictions.

Where do your convictions fit within your personal self-assessment (personal, academic, career, financial, and/or giving aspirations)?

Part Eight: Askers, Seekers, and Knockers Have Great Faith

- Askers, Seekers, and Knockers Are Fearless Even When Afraid—They Don't Stop
- Askers, Seekers, and Knockers Recognize that There Is a Power Greater Than Themselves

Askers, Seekers, and Knockers Are Fearless Even When Afraid—They Don't Stop

I can hardly think of anything that makes us more uncomfortable than fear. There is the fear of failure, fear of change, fear of people, fear of speaking in public, fear of heights, fearing of flying, etc. Joyce Meyer describes fear as **F**-false **E**-evidence **A**-appearing **R**-real. Yes, fear is a powerful emotion, and it can be a paralyzing force. Don't let fear make you a member of its "fearing family." If you allow it, fear can stop you dead in your tracks. It can keep you from moving forward on your new success journey. It can deprive you of opportunities and adventures awaiting you. If you let it, fear will deny you wealth and success. Fear can ultimately steal from you the life you are intended to live. Thus, instead of letting fear become your enemy, turn that fear around and allow fear to become a powerful personal motivator in your life.

Fear is a natural emotion that has been with humankind since the beginning of creation. It is a basic human emotion with an intended purpose—the purpose of survival. Fear tells us when to be afraid, when to flee, and when to protect ourselves. Fear is an inevitable and useful part of our being. Don't be afraid of fear, and do not let it become a hindrance to you, but instead use it for its intended purpose—survival and achievement. Redirected, fear used in a positive way can become a force multiplier in your life. A force multiplier is a factor that significantly increases your effectiveness. Have you ever noticed how much energy surrounds fear? Unfortunately, we perceive this energy as negative, but that does not have to be the case. Joyce Meyer also frequently uses a phrase, "Do it afraid." It is okay to feel the fear. However, you want to take that energy from the fear and turn it into a position of power that works in your favor.

Nobody ever said you would not feel fear when faced with a challenge. You may as well come to terms with fear right now because it is always around us when we face new challenges. Each time you embark upon a new adventure, fear will be there lurking around the corner just waiting to see if you are going to avoid the new challenge or you will confront your fears and take it on with a full frontal assault and use it as a motivator and a stepping-stone to help propel you toward the next step of your journey.

Fear can be a hindrance, or it can be a motivator; the choice is yours to make. If we let it, fear will hold us back forever. If we face it, regardless of how big and insurmountable it feels, we find that we are more capable and more interesting than we ever could have imagined. Let fear become your motivator by letting it help you to see that if you do not set your life in proper order for success, you will be doomed to a life of poverty, financial struggles, and unrealized dreams, never to have achieved your capabilities. Unless you take that step, you will miss the great things life has to offer. Remember, feeling fearful is natural; allowing yourself to get stuck in one place because of fear is unnatural. Feel the fear and then move forward in spite of your fearful feelings. When you are feeling afraid, the easiest thing to do is to remain in the cocoon of fear and refuse to progress into new territory, but then you are stuck, and growth will elude you. For growth to take place, you simply must embrace your feelings and use fear as a springboard. Sometimes we have to take a leap of faith and build the airplane as we are flying. Life isn't perfect—so what? I am not promising you that every time you confront fear and choose to step out and face that fear you will be successful every time. Life just does not work that way, but you will grow from the experience, and you will be in a different place than before. Each time you face a fear, you will grow a little more with a greater satisfaction and appreciation for yourself as you are becoming a different person a little bit at a time.

Personal Individual Action: Facing Fears

Set aside some time to reflect and meditate on areas of your life where you may have allowed fear to cheat you out of pursuing an opportunity. What are you going to do about that?

ACTION GOAL

In a few simple statements, record in your journal something that you can do and will do to help you overcome your fears in a particular area or areas of your life.

Where does facing your fears fit within your personal self-assessment (personal, academic, career, financial, and/or giving aspirations)?

Askers, Seekers, and Knockers Recognize that There Is a Power Greater Than Themselves

> People see God every day, they just don't recognize Him.
>
> —Pearl Bailey

Most great, accomplished, and successful people are quick to admit that they believe that there is a creative force greater than their individual selves. Many will tell you that their success lies in their ability to tap into that source of power and allow it to lead them through great wisdom. If you want to be truly great and able to accomplish all that you were created to become, you too must be willing to connect to that creative force. Numerous researchers have found that people with religious beliefs seem to have greater life satisfaction than people with no connections to spiritual or religious belief. People who are connected to a power greater than themselves also tend to be able to cope with the challenges of life better than nonspiritual people. There is something to be said for having a strong belief system that says to you, *"You're not alone. Together we are strong, and we can accomplish the impossible no matter what comes and no matter what goes. All is well because tomorrow is a new opportunity for a new beginning."*

As you set out to build your framework for success, you too will realize that you are not alone on this new journey. The best way to achieve success is to be connected to your power source because you will need it. If you are not connected, you need to get connected. Connect to your personal source of spiritual power so that wisdom may operate and flow in your life. Connect to trusted people so that you may find encouragement. Connect to meaningful social networks so that you may find avenues to unwind. Connect to your church, synagogue, temple, or other groups so you may constantly be exhorted and encouraged to accomplish your goals. Connect to your community so you may always have opportunities to invest in others. We are better together; the Creator of this great universe never meant for us to go it alone.

As you accept and connect to the power that is greater than yourself, you will readily realize that you are more than what you see with your mere natural eyes. You will come to realize that you can accomplish great and marvelous things, too wonderful to tell. You only need to open your mind to the great possibilities. There was a time in our past when there was no thought that man could land and walk on the moon, yet Neil Armstrong did the impossible and changed our possibilities about space forever. There was a time when electricity did not exist, but Thomas Edison and Nikola Tesla changed the world by making impossibilities possible even beyond what Edison or Tesla could have dreamed. There was a time when it was impossible to perceive that a woman would travel in space, but Valentina Tereshkova (Soviet) did in 1963, Sally Ride (American) did in 1983, and Dr. Mae Carol Jemison (first African American) did in 1992.

What at one time seemed impossible and unbelievable became possible and believable by ordinary people believing that they could achieve the impossible. And so it is with your life too. What seems impossible for someone like you becomes possible when you believe the unbelievable. Need more encouragement? Review Mark 10:27, "*With God all things are possible.*" Believe that possibilities belong to you too. The Great Creator of this universe created greatness in you just as he did these people. It is up to you to create your possibilities. While you may not be able to predict your future, you can create it. You have the power to unlock your potential; you are the creator of your destiny. The key is to not give up and to keep trying. The Creator of this universe gave you consciousness and intelligence; therefore, your greatness is by choice, your choice. Wisdom is available to each and every one of us. The choice is yours to connect to that source of power that is greater than you, that source that feeds your aspirations.

Personal Individual Action: Choosing to Be Great by Connecting

Set aside some time to reflect and meditate on areas of your life where you require greater strength, wisdom, and direction. Ponder these questions. Are you connected to a power greater than yourself? Should you be? Are you connected to others for encouragement and strength? Should you be? The choice is yours to make. No one else can determine the responses to these questions for you.

ACTION GOAL

In a few simple statements, record in your journal something that you can do and will do to get connected for greater strength, wisdom, encouragement, and direction.

Where does getting connected to a power source greater than yourself and to others fit within your personal self-assessment (personal, academic, career, financial, and/or giving aspirations)?

Part Nine: Askers, Seekers, and Knockers Are Dreamers

Askers, Seekers, and Knockers Are Dreamers and They Dream Big

- Vision is Required
- Discipline is Required
- Peace is Required

Askers, Seekers, and Knockers Are Dreamers and They Dream Big

> Vision without action is just a dream, action without vision just passes the time, but vision with action can change the world.
>
> —Nelson Mandela

Dreaming big by turning your dreams into visions and your visions into your reality is a worthy endeavor! A vision without action is nothing more than daydreaming; it's time to stop daydreaming and give birth to your dreams. Your pathway to success is through your dreams and visions for your life. Look into your future. What do you see? I challenge you to see the impossible dreams about yourself and how you can accomplish them. You have the power within you to make a real difference. You are the catalyst that can affect the change that you want. How do I know this? Because I am a product of dreaming. As I mentioned, I am a farm girl who grew up in back fields of Cotton Plant, Arkansas. I grew up chopping and picking cotton, pumping water, using an outdoor toilet, and heating the house with wood heaters. I am stressing to you the power in the ability to dream and visualize about accomplishing something bigger than you ever thought you could imagine or achieve.

Your dreams will require three things: vision in order to visualize your success, discipline in order to stick with the plan, and peace with your decisions in order to enjoy the journey. On your journey to accomplishing your dreams, seek to find inspiration that will motivate you to action. I am especially inspired by a character in the Bible called Elijah found in 1 Kings 18:43-44. I see dedicated persistence at work in Elijah's life. Even at a time when Israel was living in a drought and had not seen rain for quite some time. He could see the abundance of rain in his spirit. When there wasn't a cloud in the sky, he sent his servant to look for rainclouds, and he asked him, "What do you see?" The servant went and looked six times, and each of the six times, he came back and said there was nothing to see. Elijah sent him a seventh time, and on the seventh time the servant came back and said, "I see a small cloud that is no bigger than the size of a man's hand." It was on that bit of information that Elijah moved out and acted. If Elijah had not tried the seventh time, he would have missed an opportunity to act. I have four questions for you. First, what do you see? What are your dreams? Second, will you keep looking until you get your inspiration to act on your dreams? Third, will you let your dreams and visions dry up and die inside of you? Fourth, will you let your dreams become your visions, and visions become your realities?

Don't be afraid to **dream big.** Get rid of your limiting beliefs. Your dreams should be bigger than what you by yourself can accomplish. Your family and friends may think that you have lost your mind. That's okay; dream anyway. Dream your way out of a difficult situation. Dream your way out of economic challenges. Your insight into the future has the ability to uplift you and propel you into a future you could never have imagined. Your dreams have the potential to change you, to change the direction of your life, to impact your family, your growth and development (spiritually, naturally, and physically), and your economic security. As I warned before, this will require dedication, persistence, and perseverance. It takes work to allow your dreams to take root and become your visions, and your visions your reality. If you are reading this book, you have already set your dreams in forward motion, so lean in and get busy.

VISION IS REQUIRED

A clear vision of what success is to you is required. "*Where there is no vision, the people perish*" (Proverbs 29:18). Where there is no vision, there is no guidance, no path, no direction, and no destination. When people have no real vision of themselves and who they were born to be, they can fall prey to anything that catches their eye. If people could really see their purpose for being on earth, their value and their potential, they would never allow drugs, alcohol, crime, lasciviousness, and other vices to take control of their lives. Vision is having the ability to see past the circumstances of what is standing in front of you right now and see your future possibilities. Except you are able to visualize your hopes, desires, dreams, and your destination, you will not be able to develop strategic goals and objectives and a plan of action that will propel you toward your dreams. Having a solid vision for your life will bring you the necessary discipline and focus you need to avoid getting distracted from your success journey.

Every journey requires the ability to see those things that be not as though they already exist (Romans 4:17). Against all hope, you can dare to hope and see the impossibilities as possibilities. Let your hope serve as the substance of those things that have not yet manifested in your life. Let your hope serve as your anchor to keep you from wandering from your path. If your visions were not possible for you to accomplish them, they would have never been birthed in your spirit. Your hope is the key ingredient that drives you, inspires you, and motivates you to action. Your hope is the evidence that your visions are possible. You are to no longer consider your own weaknesses or your disadvantages, but instead have faith in your abilities to accomplish this journey. Constantly connect with your purpose that the Great Creator hid inside of you at the moment you were conceived. Speak life into your visions; never allow your tongue to speak negatively about yourself, your dreams, or your visions. Get rid of the self-doubt. If you do not believe in your dreams and visions, who will?

I have one more Bible story from the Book of Numbers 13-14 that I hope will inspire you to action and help you to see that sometimes you may stand alone, but stand anyway. Don't get discouraged because others do not see what you see. The dream is not given to them, but to you. Joshua and Caleb were two men who were part of a twelve-member spy team that Moses sent out to assess the land of Canaan. Ten of the spies came back afraid and complaining. Even though they saw promise and great opportunities in the new land, they let the obstacles, challenges, and barriers dissuade them. They complained about the fortified city, they complained about the size of the people, and they lost their focus. Blinded by the obstacles, challenges, and the barriers to their success, they were willing to give up and settle for a life of complacency and drag the rest of the community with them. But Joshua and Caleb came back saying things like, "Yes, there are obstacles we will have to overcome. Yes, we will face challenges. Yes, we will have to make sacrifices, and yes, we will have to remove barriers, but did you see the size of those giant grapes?" They believed the land offered exceptional opportunities for all. They shouted back to the crowd, "Come on, men. We can do this, we have the Great Creator guiding us!"

Regardless of the circumstance you may encounter, you are capable of achieving success. Regardless of the barriers you may face, you are capable of achieving this success. Reset your vision to see beyond the challenges. What about you? Will you be a Joshua and Caleb, or will you be like the rest of the crowd? What are you letting block and fade out your visions? Do you see discrimination? Do you see a lack of opportunities? Do you see a difficult boss or coworkers? Do you see a lack of education? Do you see a lack of finances? Do you see illness? Do you see a jail or prison record? Do you see a lost opportunity? Do you see family brokenness? What are your barriers that are keeping you from the promised land of empowerment? See the barrier that is obstructing your dreams and visions, and set your sights on doing something about it. Do what is within your control to do.

DISCIPLINE IS REQUIRED

Accomplishing your dreams will not be an easy task; this is hard work. It will require personal self-discipline. You will encounter many barriers and setbacks; dream anyway. You will encounter discouragement; dream anyway. You will encounter locked doors; dream anyway. There will sometimes be false starts; dream anyway. The greater the dream, the greater the cost. Your dream is going to cost you something; dream anyway. Your dream is not just about you. Your dream will not only elevate you, but it will elevate others whose lives you touch, your children, your spouse, friends, neighbors, associates, coworkers. Those you lead and those you follow will be inspired by your tenacity. You cannot allow public opinion or negative people to drop poison words in your spirit to cloud your vision. Against all odds, have faith in your skills, your abilities, and the promise of your purpose. There is no way around it. You must commit to self-discipline if you want your dreams and visions to be realized. Your intellectual senses may be screaming at you that this is nonsense. Tell your senses to quiet down. You will never gain the discipline you need over your life until you gain discipline over your thought processes. Let your dreams and visions become the defining moments of your life, not negative words and thoughts.

Remember, those goals and objectives associated with your personal individual actions will require stick-to-it-ness. Discipline is the key to successfully achieving those goals and objectives. You will need to practice discipline every day. Focus on getting results that are specific and measurable so that you will be able to document your steady progress. You may at times feel like giving up, but don't. There are millions of people who never accomplished their dreams because they gave up too soon. Sometimes success was just around the bend in the road. No matter what you may encounter, the essential point is that you stay focused, keep your discipline, and keep moving forward. Recognize what may have contributed to your setback, correct the situation, and get back on the path of your journey. Remember what Millie would say, "*Don't should on yourself.*" You have a source of strength, and you need to continually tap into it through prayer, meditation, and showing gratitude. The Great Creator has not left you alone on your journey. A.S.K. for wisdom, guidance, and direction. Remember, *there is no growth in the comfort zone, and no comfort in the growth zone.* While you may not be able to predict your future, you can take control and create it. It's time to get out of the safety of the familiar and grow.

PEACE IS REQUIRED

Your success journey will require you to have peace about your decisions and the choices you make. This journey can become demanding and overwhelming at times. Without your peace, you will find no joy in sticking with your dreams or with this journey. If your mind is troubled and you are in constant turmoil, reexamine your thoughts, choices, and decision. The true measure of your success journey will be found in your peace and the joy that springs from that peace. Let peace and joy be your companions on this journey, and they will help keep you in a state of balance and well-being. Having peace does not equate to a life without challenges and difficulties, but it does mean you have the ability to choose to be joyful through your journey. Your joy is strengthened by finding peace with your internal faith and not focusing on external things which are fleeting. When you allow peace and joy to be your companions on this journey, you will find happiness in some of the smaller pleasures of life. Celebrate with family, friends, and accountable partners frequently. Be grateful and give thanks for small accomplishments, peace of mind, a balanced life, and new experiences. If you find that you are experiencing more and more times of stress and frustration, you may want to increase your meditation time and allow the quietness to settle your thoughts. Mediation is a great way to regain self-control over your mental thoughts and well-being. If you made a decision or a choice that is continually brothering you, follow your internal feelings and allow your intuition to guide you on the matter. Never allow the woes of the world to steal away your peace and joy. Happiness comes in spurts, but peace and joy is a way of life. You can actively choose peace and joy for your life every day.

STORY TIME
Ajaye's Story: A Fatherless Son
He always knew he had the gift to inspire and motivate others; unfortunately, that gift was hidden behind the tough exterior of a child growing up fatherless. Nevertheless, Ajaye' overcame his own self-defeating demons and found his path to his dream of becoming a motivational speaker/life coach, author, and certified member of the John Maxwell Team.

Ajaye' Carter grew up in South Central Los Angeles, California, in the 1960s and 1970s without his father being a major part of his life, and that experience left an indelible imprint on him. During that time, his life was influenced by the pictures displayed on daily television, which included race riots and the civil unrest that led to the Civil Rights Movement, demonstrations, assassinations of President John F. Kennedy, Robert F. Kennedy, and Dr. Martin Luther King, Jr., gang violence, daily drive-by shootings that led to 10:00 p.m. curfews, etc. He grew up being raised by a single mother in a home with himself and his sister. Ajaye' had a difficult life, and often there was very little money for clothes, shoes, and other life necessities. Throughout his life, Ajaye' remembers being teased and called Patches because of the many patches his mother ironed onto his clothes to cover the holes he had worn into his hand-me-downs. He remembers using masking tape to hold his tennis shoes together and using cardboard inserts that outlined his foot in his shoes as shoe soles. For many years, Christmas came in February for his family, and Ajaye' thanked God for the lay-a-way plan which made it possible for his mother to afford the few Christmas gifts that she gave to them in February. Because he was often teased growing up, he suffered from a very low self-esteem. School was a struggle for him, and because he was not a very strong student, getting through elementary and high school was a difficult challenge. Ajaye' was often bullied through most of his early school years, which further contributed to his sense of low self-worth.

Although Ajaye's mother did the best she could by keeping him involved in summer camps, Cub Scouts, and various sports programs where there were numerous male role models, Ajaye' rejected most of their guidance because they were not his father. All he ever wanted, all he ever needed was his father. Because his father was absent from his life, as a young child Ajaye' set out to look for a father's validation, love, brotherhood, a sense of manhood, and acceptance in other external relationships. He found himself gravitating to other people in the streets whom he felt would protect and guide him and fill the void missing in his life. These people became his big brothers, providers, and protectors. Following this path, led Ajaye' down a path of trouble, gang activities, drug use, alcohol, and many, many fights. His nickname became Evil Al. By the time Ajaye' reached high school, he was no longer being bullied; he had now become the bully, guided by his street big brothers. He had developed a notorious reputation as a fighter, and he enjoyed the recognition that his negative reputation brought him. Even though ill placed, this was his first recognition: he had the gift to attract and lead others.

Even though Ajaye' was in and out of trouble, there was always something within him where he also found himself being drawn to children who were from families with two parents and what he considered as good homes. He would try to become a part of their stories and try to live their dreams. If they were good athletes, he found himself following after them and trying to live and mimic their dreams for their lives. If they played football or ran track, he tried that sport instead of pursuing the sport he was best at, which was baseball. During a Little League baseball game, at the age of six, Ajaye' turned a triple play as the shortstop, so he knew baseball was his strength. He admits he grew up following after other people's dreams because, at that time, he did not have enough self-esteem, courage, and discipline to realize that he could have pursued dreams of his own.

A major turning point came in Ajaye's life when he found himself one more time in a courtroom facing the wrath of a judge. But on this particular occasion Ajaye' was given an option of either going to jail on his next brush with the law or to join the military. He opted for the latter. Even though he joined the military (US Navy), Ajaye' took his bad attitude and other mental demons with him into the military. He was difficult to get along with and often hid behind the "race card" when he failed to properly prepare himself or to successfully accomplish a task set before him.

A second major turning point came in Ajaye's life after a year in the Navy when two influential sailors (Elliot Simpson and Clarence Peters) took him aside, read him the riot act, and took him under their wings to teach, mentor, and coach him. The first valuable lesson they taught him was to stop playing the victim by throwing down the "race card" and using discrimination as an excuse for his own lack of education and self-development. They taught him to instead look internally to see what he could have done better in a particular situation. This was Ajaye's first realization that it is his character that is the most important thing that would define his life, not his reputation.

As he proceeded through the military, Ajaye' was forced to come face-to-face with his mental demons that were holding him back and keeping him trapped in a rut. He was forced to realize that as an E-5, leading other seamen, he was a horrible leader and had no role models to glean experience from. While he believed he was doing a great job because he and his team were meeting all of their requirement, his team found him to be a corrosive and disruptive leader who led through screaming, shouting, fear, and intimidation. All he knew was to impersonate the behavior of his past boot camp instructor who led a company of eighty-four individuals from all walks of life. To help him deal with his poor leadership skills, the Navy sent him to leadership, education, and development training. This course opened his eyes and his mind to the important attributes that make an effective leader. This school taught him a lot about himself, his own blind spots, and about the behaviors he needed to change, delete, and improve to become an effective situational leader.

Because Ajaye' lacked mature judgment and was ill-prepared to deal with life and finances, an insurance inheritance from the death of his mother at the age of thirty and the death of his father two years later only contributed to his poor life choices, which had a devastating impact on his ability to advance in his military career. As a young African American male who did not have the finest things in life, he did not help his self-image as he used much of his inheritance to purchase for himself a Mercedes Benz and then quickly turned it into a "tricked-out ride" with a gold package, tinted windows, telephone, and TV. He then procured for himself an assortment of Mr. T-styled gold chains, high-priced watches and rings, which he readily sported for recognition. Little did he realize that even though he had the training and necessary qualification for advancement in the military, it was his own stereotypical image, behaviors, and self-defeating attitude that held him back from advancing in the military while he watched his peers climb the ladder of success and get promoted. After failing to advance beyond the position of an E-6 and failing to reach the position of E-7 chief petty officer, after twenty years of service, Ajaye' was honorably discharged from the Navy. After leaving the military, he later found out that because of the image he portrayed, unbeknownst to himself, he was under constant surveillance by the military as a possible drug dealer. It was at that moment that he realized he had been his own worst enemy and that it was his poor image that had sabotaged his military career.

A third major turning point in Ajaye's life came in July 1993 after the death of a young close friend. Ajaye' took his last drink of alcohol and entered himself into an alcohol rehabilitation program. This is where he started to turn his life around. Ajaye' had slowly come to realize that he too had dreams and visions for his life and knew he wanted to be greater than he was but was struggling with knowing how to achieve his dreams. He also knew that he gained energy from being around people, and he knew that he had a strong desire to lead and inspire others. This realization really hit home for him at his military retirement ceremony. Ajaye' was expecting a crowd of about thirty people when well over one hundred people showed up, all expressing appreciation for him and how he had inspired them in some way. He was inspired, and he knew that he needed to take control of his own destiny and pursue this dream.

Ajaye' finally realized that he needed vision, discipline, and peace in his life. He began to perfect his vision for his life after fifteen years of chasing a dream that did not come true. He learned you cannot become successful in life looking and living in the rearview mirror and trying to live other people's dreams. He decided that he would start by changing his life and the people around him. He knew he needed to see himself differently by seeing his own potential. He enrolled in Southern Illinois University, where he completed three years of study. Since that time, Ajaye' has transferred his skills from the military to a successful career within the federal government, where he now holds several certifications in his profession as a certified civil rights trainer/investigator. As Ajaye' began to assess himself and focus on his life's purpose and on what he really wanted out of life, his real vision and dreams for his life began to emerge. He began to live by the philosophy "Winning from within" by overcoming the enemy (his subconscious) and by getting rid of all the negative self-talk that sabotaged his life's dreams and career goals. He further realized that if he was to walk in his dreams, he would have to get out of his comfort zone, make the necessary sacrifices, and be willing to pay the price for achieving his dreams, and that is exactly what Ajaye' has done. He now lives by the motto "Attitude is everything: fix it or kick it!" In the words of his mentor Keith Harrell, "Your attitude today will determine your altitude tomorrow!"

He made the life-changing decision to pursue his dream of becoming a world-class motivational speaker/life coach, an author, and a certified member of the John Maxwell Team, adding value to people and organizations. The key to his success was to surround himself over the past ten years with individuals who have accomplished what he desires. Some of those successful individuals include John C. Maxwell, Les Brown, Jack Canfield, Willie Jolley, Johnny Wimbrey, the late Keith Harrell, Zig Ziglar, and Jim Rohn.

Ajaye' readily admits that this new focus for his life took significant discipline. To pursue his dreams, Ajaye' has spent and continues to spend countless hours perfecting his craft. He continuously invests in self-improvement and training opportunities with some of the world's top motivators and trainers. He has not only made significant sacrifices on his time, but he has invested financially to pursue his dreams. He clearly understands the concept that *your dreams will cost you something and you must be willing to pay the price.*

Today, Ajaye' has significantly transformed his life. He is not only living his dream of becoming a motivational speaker and life coach, but he is also an author of the book *I Mastered Failure, But Look at Me Now!* Through his life story he has encouraged thousands of individuals to step out of their comfort zones and pursue their visions and dreams. His journey to success has not been an easy ride, but the story of his success is one of inspiration and encouragement to every individual who is facing their own challenges, mental demons, and self-defeating behaviors. His compelling life story is a stirring call to action to all who desire to turn their challenges into triumphs. Sought after by various entities, his message has encouraged thousands across the corporate, public, government, and academia regarding organizational success, personal achievement, and professional excellence. Ajaye' Carter is the president and CEO of Career Image-Consultants http://www.career-image-consultants.com. An expert in human behavior modification and a well-known master facilitator, he has a unique ability to educate, inspire, and involve audience members in his powerful interactive seminars.

Ajaye' is at peace with his decision to pursue his dreams. In spite of the challenges, setbacks, and sacrifices, Ajaye' has found great joy and satisfaction in pursuing his dreams. As he now looks back at the challenges that he went through in his life, he realizes that these challenges were preparing him to pursue his own dreams. He realized that these challenges did not come to destroy him but to make him stronger. However, he readily admits that the choice was his to make. In the words of Ajaye, "*Success is a do-it-yourself project.*" Pursuing his dreams has allowed him to accomplish his life goals and to turn his dreams into reality. He says that life is your DOOR to opportunity; it is your Duty, Opportunity, Obligation, and Responsibility. Ajaye' believes that success in life has very little to do with how you start out, but about how you FINISH! He encourages everyone to "choose to win big!"

According to Ajaye', everyone goes through tough times. He believes it is his job as a motivator to help people move past their excuses and find their own inner warrior. He has firsthand knowledge that once you stop making excuses, you will start creating the life you have always wanted. To book Ajaye' as a speaker or to learn more about his *No More Excuses* speaking tour, go to www.CoachAjCarter. com or e-mail him at CoachAjCarter@ajayecarter.com.

Personal Individual Action: Dream, Dream, Dream

Set aside some time to reflect and meditate on the dreams and visions you have for your life. Do not be afraid to dream and dream big. Continue to imagine and picture in your mind what you want your life to be. Dream about what success will look like when you achieve it. This is not a single success. I am speaking about many different areas of success on many different levels in your life. Whatever you want your life to be, you should be dreaming about that every day because visualizing success with your mind's eyes can be a potent exercise that can significantly impact your expectations. These are your thoughts, beliefs, and visions about your life. Let yourself go as you dream. What might you dream and visualize about for yourself when you are not worried about anyone else seeing your thoughts? How do you see yourself if there were no challenges holding you back? It's not foolish, it's not frivolous, it's not impossible, and it's not too late no matter what your age or circumstances are. A word of caution here: this is not an assessment of seeing how another person views you or you depending on another person to change your life. This is not about thinking that someone is going to ride in on a white horse, swoop you up, and carry you off into the sunset. This is about you changing your own expectations and your own circumstances. This is about the self-control that you have and the discipline that you exercise in your own life.

ACTION GOAL

In a few simple statements, record in your journal something that you can do and will do to put you on the path to realizing your dreams and visions.

Where do your dreams and visions fit within your personal self-assessment (personal, academic, career, financial, and/or giving aspirations)?

Part Ten: Awakening to Take Action

- Askers, Seekers, and Knockers Get Up, Get Busy, and Change Their Circumstances
- Complete The Post Personal Self-Assessment
- Developing Your Personal Plan of Action
- Your New Personal Journey Begins
- Creating Your Personal Plan of Action, Your Personal Goals and Objectives

Charts
  - Personal Aspirations
  - Academic Aspirations
  - Career Aspirations
  - Financial Aspirations
  - Giving Aspirations

Askers, Seekers, and Knockers Get Up, Get Busy, and Change Their Circumstances

> Strength and growth come only through continuous effort and struggle.
>
> —Napoleon Hill

Now that you are fired up and ready to go, as President Barack Obama would say, let's have the talk about obstructions. There are going to be life challenges presented as obstructions that will come out of nowhere designed to stop you from taking and completing your journey to success. Obstructions are an inescapable part of life; accept this truth. This is the universe testing your resolve and your commitment for this journey. It is important that you clearly understand that these obstructions that spring up are meant to strengthen you, not stop you. Face them, resolve them, and move forward. There are two important obstructions you must accept.

The first is fear. We talked about this earlier. You will be afraid to step out of your comfort zone and face the fear of the unknown. Frequently reread the section "Askers, Seekers, and Knockers Are Fearless Even When Afraid—They Don't Stop" for sustained encouragement. Find comfort in knowing that everyone who has ever set out on a new journey to change their life has felt fear. Not only will you face fear, but you will have to face a lot of what-ifs. "What if I don't have the resources? What if my spouse leaves me? What if I do all of this and things still do not get better? What if I can't read and write very well? What if I have a record? What if my health gets worse?" Be like the great ones and don't let the fear of the what-ifs arrest you and pull you off your journey to a life of success.

The second is life itself. Life happens, and it will present itself almost every day in the form of one obstruction or another. You will have some good days, and you will have some challenging days. However, it's like the song says, your good days will outweigh your bad days, if you keep your peace. The challenges of life will not stop simply because you have decided to move your life to a higher level. In fact, you can expect to see even more obstructions designed to pull you off your journey, but remember, these challenges are sent to make you stronger.

Some obstructions will be within your control to eliminate, and some will not. Those obstructions which you have the power to fix or eliminate, do it. Those you can't fix, find a way to maneuver around them and keep leaning forward. Remember the Serenity Prayer. Pray it frequently and mean it! *"Lord, grant me the serenity to accept the things I cannot change, the courage to change the things I can, and the wisdom to know the difference."* Don't let life's obstructions get you bogged down in things that you have no control over. But at the same time, don't become a coward either and not fix those things that you do have control over. The wisdom in knowing the difference between the two is essential to your success. You have within your control the power to fix that which is broken in your life. Now is the time for you to be strong and very courageous. Don't stop, don't quit, don't turn around; you are already on the road to prosperity in every area of your life.

The Great Creator of the universe gave us many parables on earth to live by so that we may be strengthen for the journey. Let's observe one of them as a source of reassurance that we can overcome obstructions. Let's equate the birth of your new journey to that of the life of a tree as illustrated by the biosphere project. Around the early 1990s, the biosphere project, some refer to it as the bio-dome experiment, was conducted in the Arizona desert. The scientists were attempting to construct perfect living conditions for both man, animals, and plant life. The experiment failed miserably in numerous areas mostly because life is not perfect and without common life struggles, there is no real development and resilience. For example, trees did not respond well in the bio-dome because there were no external forces pushing against them forcing them to grow stronger. The scientists surprisingly found that as new trees grew and developed, they required the force of nature such as the wind and rain to strengthen them in order to withstand the storms that are sure to come. Thus, as the trees grew, they simply toppled over when they grew to a certain length. Although trees are resilient, it is the pressures of nature that contribute to that resilience. The experiment revealed that it takes the force of the wind and the rain blowing against trees from the time they are very young, causing them to sway back and forth, for the trees to develop a strong trunk and a deep root system capable of supporting the trees' height and weight. Without this source of strain on trees, they will be underdeveloped and weak. A strong trunk and root system is needed so that trees will not be uprooted and fall over under the force of natural storms.

Just as it is with trees, so is it with humans. Your obstructions are there to help strengthen your endurance so that you may build strong root systems capable of sustaining you during the storms of life. During dry seasons, trees also rely on their deep and complex root systems to draw out water that is buried deep in the earth. You too will experience some dry season in your life when it seems as though your plans are not flourishing. It is during the dry seasons of your life that you will need to reach down deep in your inner spirit and draw energy and strength from your faith, convictions, and commitments in order to overcome life obstructions. We all dream of a perfect life without challenges, conflicts, troubles, and other obstructions, but then we would find that we are weak creatures incapable of survival unless we have been tested and developed. Pope Paul VI said, *"All life demands struggle. Those who have everything given to them become lazy, selfish, and insensitive to the real values of life. The very striving and hard work that we so constantly try to avoid is the major building block in the person we are today."* Though we do not like obstructions, it is during the periods of overcoming these obstructions that we develop the strength and endurance needed for sustainment when life challenges us. Our strength and ability to endure is increased through times of struggles.

One more point about obstructions. I am going to challenge your thinking about obstructions. When we hear the word *obstruction*, we automatically see it as negative. Beware, not every obstruction is negative; some are very positive and needed as supplements to your journey. Nevertheless, if you are not focused, disciplined, and persistent about your ultimate goal, you could find such comfort in the positive obstructions, that you could wander too long, if not permanently, from the real path to your overarching success. Don't become distracted too long in a comforting situation, albeit may be good for you; if it is not the end of your journey, get back on the path.

Complete the Post-Personal Self-Audit

Post-Personal Self-Audit

Note whether there are any new insights, revelations, or changes in your responses since reading this book.

Who Are You? What Is Your Spiritual Name?

This is a discovery question. Try to answer this question without stating your name, race, ethnicity, national origin, gender, profession, heritage, occupation, or status in life. Your true spiritual name is tied to your purpose, the reason why you were born. When you were conceived in your mother's womb, your name was placed deep in your spirit to be searched out by you. The search for your true spiritual name will take you on your personal journey of discovery. You will be required to search your heart, your spirit, and your life for this answer. Quietly look for the common thread that has always been present within you. The thing which vibrates your spirit and quickens your life. Don't worry if you cannot answer this question at this time. More will be revealed as you read through the book that will better prepare you to respond to this question as you take this new journey.

If you were able to answer the above question, list your spiritual name below. How and when did you discover the real you or your spiritual name?

_____

_____

Any new insights?

_____

Personal Aspirations: Where Are You and Where Do You Want to Be?

1. Where are you physically—your location (state, city, neighborhood, etc.)?

    _____

    Is this where you want to be? _____ Yes _____ No
    If not, where do you want to be? _____

    _____

    What is holding you back from being where you want to be?

    _____

Any new insights? _____

2. Where are you emotionally? _____
    Is this a good place for you? _____ Yes _____ No
    If not, where do you want to be emotionally? _____

    _____

    What is holding you back from being where you want to be?

    _____

Any new insights? _____

3.   Where are you spiritually?

      Is this where you want to be? _____ Yes _____ No

If not, where do you want to be spiritually? _____

_____

What is holding you back from being where you want to be?

_____

Any new insights? _____

4.   Where are you in your personal life (married, divorced, single, with children, etc.)?

_____

_____

      Is this where you want to be? _____ Yes _____ No

If not, where do you want to be in your personal life?

_____

_____

What is holding you back from being where you want to be?

_____

_____

Any new insights? _____

5.   Are there relationships in your life that you should change?

      _____ Yes _____ No

If yes, why should they be changed? _____

_____

What is holding you back from making this change?

_____

Any new insights? _____

6.   Are there relationships in your life that should be restored or established?

                                            _____ Yes _____ No

        If yes, why are these relationships important to you? _____
_____

        What is holding you back from establishing or restoring these relationships? _____
_____
_____

Any new insights? _____

Academic Aspirations: Where Are You and Where Do You Want to Be?

7.   Where are you in your academic life? _____
            Is this where you want to be? _____ Yes _____ No
        If not, where do you want to be? _____
_____

        What is holding you back from being where you want to be?
_____
_____

Any new insights? _____

Career Aspirations: Where Are You and Where Do You Want to Be?

8.   Where are you in your career/professional life? _____
            Is this where you want to be? _____ Yes _____ No

If not, where do you want to be? _____

_____

What is holding you back from being where you want to be?

_____

_____

Any new insights? _____

Financial Aspirations: Where Are You and Where Do You Want to Be?

9. Where are you in your financial circumstances?
    Is this where you want to be? _____ Yes _____ No
    If not, where do you want to be? _____

    _____

    What is holding you back from being where you want to be?

    _____

    _____

Any new insights? _____

Investing in the Lives of Others: Where Are You and Where Do You Want to Be?

10. Are you predisposed to helping others such as through charities, tithing, volunteering, etc.?

    _____ Yes _____ No
    If no, do you feel it is not important to give your time, energy, and/or money to help others? _____

    _____

    _____

What is preventing you from giving/investing in the lives of others?

_____

Any new insights? _____

Compare the pre-personal assessment and the post-personal assessment. Review the below questions. Did you gain any new insights regarding your responses from the time prior to reading the book and after reading the book? Note any differences.

- Have you counted the cost (tangible and intangible) of getting your life on the track you want it to be on?
- Have you counted the cost (tangible and intangible) of not getting your life on track with what you want?
- Assess which cost is greater.
- Does the greater cost impact others besides you?

Developing Your Personal Plan of Action

> The future belongs to those who believe in the beauty of their dreams.
>
> —Eleanor Roosevelt

Your personal journey begins! It is now time to start developing your personal plan of action (PPA) that will get you from where you are today to where you want to be tomorrow personally, spiritually, academically, and professionally through the process of ASKing. ASKing for what you want is not a substitute for doing. ASKing is action operating at its best.

First, review the responses contained in your pre-personal self-assessment. This is the starting point for developing your goals and objectives which make up the content of your personal plan of action. The bottom line is, if you do not like what your pre-personal self-assessment revealed to you, you must do something to change your circumstances. The assessment phase of ASKing is not a small undertaking; it is serious and requires great effort. But if you are serious about creating success in your life, this process is necessary.

Second, complete the post-personal self-assessment. Review and compare the responses contained in the pre- and post-assessments. If you noted any differences in your responses between the two personal assessments, what do you think contributed to the difference in your responses? Did you gain any new insight about yourself as you read through the book? Note what contributed to your new insight.

Review again the principles of A.S.K. found in Matthew 7:7-8, *"Ask, and it shall be given to you; Seek, and you shall find; Knock and it will be opened to you. Everyone who asks receives, he who seeks finds, and to him who knocks it will be opened."* Remember, do not confuse this scripture with only natural desires, items, things, or any other thing of a material worth or value. Some of us have been taught to just simply believe for something, have faith, meditate, quote a few Bible verse, fall down on our knees, pray, and ask God for it, and then poof, just like magic, it will appear or work out somehow in our favor. We wrongly believe that the only investment on our part is to just believe and achieve it, no other investment required. This type of wrong thought pattern has crippled many individuals and robbed them of their purpose and of many opportunities that could have brought them to great success in life. I will challenge you that if your interpretation of the above scripture is for material gain only, it is an incorrect interpretation. What has worked for me is taking the principles of Matthew 7:7-8—Asking, Seeking, and Knocking—and adding it to faith and then channeling that faith into dedicated, persistent, and deliberate actions designed to bring results. Following that method, A.S.K. will manifest as extraordinary success in your life and will bring with it great satisfaction, joy, and peace.

Your New Personal Journey Begins

> Two roads diverged in the woods, and I took the one less traveled, and that has made all the difference.
>
> —Robert Frost

By now you have completed the pre-personal self-assessment, you have completed the book, you have created several personal individual actions, and you have completed the post-personal self-assessment. You are ready to begin the process of discovering the real you, your purpose for being here, and obtaining your successful life as you have defined it to be. My greatest hope for you during this entire process is that you discover the real you without giving your given name or any other external identifiers. Now let's talk about where you are in your life and your plans to get you where you want to be tomorrow. This journey will not be a short trip, so don't get discouraged.

Askers Develop a Personal Plan of Action Aimed at Achieving Success

It's time to design your plan, develop your strategies, direct your effort, and focus your energy. In developing your personal plan of action, it will be important to have a clear picture of what success looks like to you. Is it getting your dream job, achieving a certain level of financial independence, a certain academic degree, a certain profession? Remember, success for one person may not necessarily be success for another. Remember that A.S.K. is a continuous effort. You are assessing yourself at the level of where you are now; later when you actually achieve the level of success you identified in this plan, you will again go through the A.S.K. for a different level of success you want to achieve.

The most important thing about developing your personal plan for success is identifying and developing goals and objectives that will propel you toward achieving the level of success you have identified. If you are still unfamiliar with how to develop personal goals and objectives, I recommend that you rely on resources that will help you develop your goals and objectives. There are numerous resources on the market that will guide you through creating journals, creating goals and objectives, and creating vision boards. If you need help in these areas, take advantage of these resources. Visit your local bookstore or Amazon.com to seek out such resources. Depending on what you identified in your self-assessments, you may find it necessary to seek professional guidance in dealing with some of the areas of your life. If you identify this as a necessity, I encourage you to invest in yourself and seek the assistance you require. As you identify areas that you want to accomplish or make improvement in, make specific goals and develop objectives and milestone.

Create Visuals

Why create visuals? Creating visuals to help you visualize the manifestation of your dreams, visions, goals and objectives is a powerful tool. Throughout my various journeys, I find it most helpful to journal, develop goals and objectives, and create vision boards with pictures, affirmations, quotes, etc. Creating various visualizations will help you keep your long-term and short-term goals and objectives before your eyes every day. We become what we think about all day long. Visualization works by bringing to life in our spirits those things that have not yet manifested in our natural existence. I have used vision boards to help me accomplish several goals in my life. I have found that my inner vibrations are activated more powerfully when I can see in pictures what my success looks like long before it happens. Habakkuk 2:2-3 says, *"And the Lord answered me and said, Write the vision, and make it plain upon tables that he may run that read it. For the vision is yet for an appointed time, but at the end it shall speak, and not lie: though it tarry, wait for it; because it will surely come, it will not tarry."* This will allow you to keep before you pictures of your dreams and where you are headed.

Why journal? This is your personal collection of thoughts, reflections, concerns, and achievements. Journaling will help you get things out of your head and down on paper so that you may have better mental clarity about what you are facing. It is a way of cataloguing, charting, and monitoring the steps and progress of your journey. It also allows you to establish a record of your life as a reminder to you that you are capable and able to achieve your desires. It also establishes a memorial record for others to read after you are no longer in this earth. Perhaps your family will be inspired and have a better understanding of what inspired, drove, and motivated you to make certain decisions and follow certain paths in life.

Why create goals and objectives? Your goals and objectives are the keys to all of this. Your goals and objectives will point you in the right direction and keep you on track. The process of creating your goals and objectives is a powerful tool that brings clarity to what you are thinking about and what you want for your life. Your goals and objectives will become your true north by keeping you on the right path, especially when life obstructions interfere with your journey.

Creating Your Personal Plan of Action, Your Personal Goals and Objectives

> It is when things go hardest, when life becomes most trying, that there is greatest need for having a fixed goal.
>
> —Bertie Charles Forbes

Go to the Personal Plan of Action chart. This is where you will fill in your goals and objectives and timelines. It is critically important to assign a timeline to each goal, objective, and milestone. Make your goals, objectives, and milestones specific enough so that you can identify when you successfully accomplish one. As you develop your goals and objectives, create pictures to align with your overarching goals. For example, if one of your goals is to own a luxury car, obtain pictures or a miniature toy model of the car you desire, a Mercedes, a Audi, a BMW, a truck, a Cadillac, or whatever your dream luxury car is. Develop a goals book or a goals chart or a vision board. Ensure that you review your goals, objectives, and milestones routinely. Always chart the manifestation of accomplishments and achievements. As you develop your goals, objectives, and milestones, build into the structure a reminder to practice celebrating accomplishments and achievements no matter how small or how great. The purpose of the celebration is to mark a joyous event that happens in your life. Documenting your celebration will also serve as a motivator for you, and it will serve to encourage you to continue on your journey of success. Celebrate with others if you like, but you can also celebrate with yourself. Okay, let's create your personal plan of action!

Relying on your responses from the below documents, let's create and execute your personal plan of action:

- Pre-personal self-assessment
- Personal individual actions
- List of goals and objectives
- Post-personal self-assessment

Don't rush this process. Take the appropriate amount of time to develop your strategic goals and objectives. Your personal plan of action will become your road map for this exciting journey you have decided to take that will get you from where you are today to where you want to be tomorrow. This plan should be detailed enough to keep you on track and to alert you when you get off track. Go to your chart and start filling in your goals and objectives. Note: it is not required that you follow the goal charts provided as you may prefer to develop your own goals chart.

An action plan is nothing without execution!

CHARTS

Personal Plan of Action (PPA) charts

1. Personal Aspirations
2. Academic Aspirations
3. Career Aspirations
4. Financial Aspirations
5. Giving Aspirations

Your Personal Journey Begins with Your Personal Plan of Action (PPA)

Starting from Where I am Today to Change Where I Want to Be Tomorrow

"There Is No Comfort in the Growth Zone and No Growth in the Comfort Zone." (Author unknown)

PERSONAL ASPIRATIONS EXAMPLE	Target Date	Objectives: Things I must do on my journey to achieving my personal aspirations	Target Date	Remarks/Status
GOAL 1: Purchase a home that meets the needs of my family, (safe neighborhood, 4 bedrooms, 3 bathrooms, 2-car garage, large kitchen, large area for the children to play in)	June 2018	Examine finances, set up a budget, research realtors, research and visit possible locations, apply for bank loan, start the search.	June 2017 through June 2018	I will consistently stick to my budget and to the plans.
Challenges that require addressing:			A time of celebration:	
Challenges that require addressing:			A time of celebration:	

235

Challenges that require addressing:		A time of celebration:	
Challenges that require addressing:		A time of celebration:	

Your Personal Journey Begins with Your Personal Plan of Action (PPA)
Starting from Where I am Today to Change Where I Want to Be Tomorrow
"There Is No Comfort in the Growth Zone and No Growth in the Comfort Zone." (Author unknown)

ACADEMIC ASPIRATIONS EXAMPLE	Target Date	Objectives: Things I must do on my journey to achieving my academic aspirations	Target Date	Remarks/Status
GOAL 1: Obtain my bachelor of science degree in nursing (BSN)	May 2021	Identify a college/university, make application and get accepted, start classes.	Jan 2017 March 2017 Fall 2017	I will continually study, work hard, and get good grades. I will enroll semester after semester until this goal is completed. I will successfully graduate on time in May 2021.
Challenges that require addressing:				A time of celebration:
Challenges that require addressing:				A time of celebration:

Challenges that require addressing:		A time of celebration:	
Challenges that require addressing:		A time of celebration:	

Your Personal Journey Begins with Your Personal Plan of Action (PPA)

Starting from Where I am Today to Change Where I Want to Be Tomorrow

"There Is No Comfort in the Growth Zone and No Growth in the Comfort Zone." (Author unknown)

CAREER ASPIRATIONS	Target Date	Objectives: Things I must do on my journey to achieving my career aspirations	Target Date	Remarks/Status
Challenges that require addressing:			A time of celebration:	
Challenges that require addressing:			A time of celebration:	

Challenges that require addressing:		A time of celebration:	
Challenges that require addressing:		A time of celebration:	

Your Personal Journey Begins with Your Personal Plan of Action (PPA)
Starting from Where I am Today to Change Where I Want to Be Tomorrow
"There Is No Comfort in the Growth Zone and No Growth in the Comfort Zone." (Author unknown)

FINANCIAL ASPIRATIONS	Target Date	Objectives: Things I must do on my journey to achieving my financial aspirations	Target Date	Remarks/Status
Challenges that require addressing:				A time of celebration:
Challenges that require addressing:				A Time of Celebration:

A time of celebration:		Challenges that require addressing:	
A Time of Celebration:		Challenges that require addressing:	

Your Personal Journey Begins with Your Personal Plan of Action (PPA)
Starting from Where I am Today to Change Where I Want to Be Tomorrow
"There Is No Comfort in the Growth Zone and No Growth in the Comfort Zone." (Author unknown)

GIVING ASPIRATIONS Impacting the Lives of Others	Target Date	Objectives: Things I must do on my journey to achieving my giving aspirations	Target Date	Remarks/Status
Challenges that require addressing:		A time of celebration:		
Challenges that require addressing:		A time of celebration:		

CAROLYN MCMILLON

Challenges that require addressing:		A time of celebration:	

244

Story Time – Short Vignettes

About the Author

Carolyn Jean McMillon is a graduate of the University of Arkansas at Pine Bluff, Webster University, the US Army Management Staff College, and the Office of Personnel Management Senior Executive Service Candidate Development Program. She began her federal career as an entry-level clerk typist and from there working her way to leadership positions throughout the Department of Defense, the Department of the Army, and the Department of Homeland Security. She is a highly acclaimed and dynamic senior leader in the federal government currently serving as an executive member of the SES cadre. She serves as the founder, leader, and mentor of ASK, a group dedicated to inspiring others to achieve their greatness. Carolyn resides in the state of Maryland.

CPSIA information can be obtained
at www.ICGtesting.com
Printed in the USA
LVHW071436111118
596719LV00015B/149/P